CHRISTIANITY ACCORDING TO
ST. JOHN ·

A Selection of the Volumes in

THE STUDIES IN THEOLOGY SERIES

CHRISTIANITY
ACCORDING TO ST. JOHN

by

W. F. HOWARD, M.A., D.D.

DUCKWORTH
3 HENRIETTA STREET, LONDON, W.C.2

First Published 1943
Reprinted 1943, 1947

PRINTED IN GREAT BRITAIN BY
THOMAS NELSON AND SONS LTD.

PREFACE

THIS book contains the eight lectures given at Oxford, by the invitation of the Principal and Council of Mansfield College, during the Hilary Term 1940, under the terms of the Dale Trust. The delay of two years in their publication is due entirely to war-time conditions and the heavy and distracting duties which were laid upon the lecturer at the very time when he was revising the typescript for the press. His first inclination was to rewrite the lectures entirely, inasmuch as a form suitable for the spoken word is not always satisfactory in a printed book. On further reflection, it seemed better to keep to the original form of lectures, as a book written about the Johannine theology would demand a systematic treatment and a detailed investigation quite out of keeping with the purpose and character of these lectures.

Eleven years ago the writer published a book, *The Fourth Gospel in Recent Criticism and Interpretation* (Epworth Press, 2nd ed. 1935 : a 3rd edition, bringing the bibliography down to date, is to appear at the end of the war). To this he must refer for the treatment of questions of introduction. On one subject he feels that insufficient attention was then given to an important result of recognizing that the Johannine writings are essentially Jewish in their background and texture of thought. More recent studies in the eschatology of the New Testament have made it necessary to attempt a fuller treatment of this aspect of their theology. It is hoped that Lecture V may help some students by suggesting lines of thought which can be carried much further than the limits of a single lecture allow.

An attempt has been made, by the addition of footnotes and a few appended notes of greater length, to supply some of the more obvious omissions in the lectures as they were originally delivered. As this book is intended to stimulate inquiry and to encourage students to " verify their references," the index supplies not only the references to Philo but also the volume and page in the Loeb edition by Colson and Whitaker, so that every passage can be studied in its context both in the Greek, and also in the English translation on the opposite page. Translations from Greek authors or from German books given in the text are sometimes taken from the standard translations, and at other times made independently.

It is unfortunate that of Bultmann's valuable commentary on St. John's Gospel only four instalments had been published before the outbreak of war, so that the introduction is not available and the exposition breaks off abruptly in the middle of the twelfth chapter. A strong divergence from Professor Bultmann's point of view on many Johannine questions does not alter the fact that the present writer, and indeed every reader of this commentary, must feel how much he owes to the learning which shines out from every page.

Three books have appeared since these lectures were given to which no reference is made in the following pages. Sir Edwyn Hoskyns has left us a great legacy in his two volumes, *The Fourth Gospel*, edited with such care by Mr. F. N. Davey. Perhaps the writer may be allowed to refer to his review of this important treatment of the theology of St. John's Gospel, which appeared in the *Journal of Theological Studies*, xlii. (1941), pages 75–81. Dr. R. H. Strachan's *The Fourth Gospel. Its Significance and Environment* (1941) is the most recent and helpful exposition. Dr. C. J. Cadoux's learned work, *The Historic Mission of Jesus* (1941) should be read for its critical attitude to the theory of "realized eschatology," which finds much more sympathetic treatment in these lectures.

To three friends I am deeply indebted for reading through the typescript in its original form and for making many valuable suggestions : the Rev. J. R. Coates, M.A., the Rev. Dr. Nathaniel Micklem, and, most of all, the Rev. Dr. H. Wheeler Robinson, to whom my debt is far greater than I can acknowledge.

Every Monday in Hilary Term during one of the severest winters within memory, when travelling was exceptionally difficult because of the war, the double journey was made between Birmingham and Oxford. But nothing can efface the memory of the kindness shown by the Principals of Mansfield College and of Regent's Park College (where the lectures were given), by their colleagues, and by many other Oxford friends. To Dr. Micklem and the Tutors of Mansfield College this little book is offered in grateful acknowledgment of the honour they conferred upon the writer when they invited him to give these Dale lectures.

W. F. H.

HANDSWORTH COLLEGE
BIRMINGHAM

treatment of the theology of St. John's Gospel, which appeared in the *Journal of Theological Studies*, xlii. (1941), pages 29-38. Dr. R. H. Strachan's *The Fourth Gospel Its Significance and Environment* (1941) is the most recent and helpful exposition. Dr. G. B. Caird's learned work, *The Historic Mission of Jesus* (1941) should be read for its critical attitude to the theory of "realized eschatology," which finds much more sympathetic treatment in these lectures.

To these friends I am deeply indebted for reading through the typescript in its original form and for making many valuable suggestions: the Rev. J. K. Coates, M.A., the Rev. Dr. Nathaniel Micklem, and, most of all, the Rev. Dr. H. Wheeler Robinson, to whom my debt is far greater than I can acknowledge. Every Monday in Hilary Term during one of the severest winters within memory, when travelling was exceptionally difficult because of the war, the double journey was made between Birmingham and Oxford. But nothing can efface the memory of the kindness shown by the Principals of Mansfield College and of Regent's Park College (where the lectures were given), by their colleagues, and by many other Oxford friends. To Dr. Micklem and the Tutors of Mansfield College this little book is offered in grateful acknowledgment of the honour they conferred upon the writer when they invited him to give these Dale lectures.

W. F. H.

Handsworth College
Birmingham

CONTENTS

CONTENTS

CHAPTER I

JOHANNINE CHRISTIANITY

TOWARDS the end of the first century a group of writings began to make their way into the Christian world which a later generation ascribed to the Apostle John. They consist of a Gospel, three Epistles, and an Apocalypse. The last of these is the only one to bear an author's name, and it is strange that there is nothing to identify this John, seer and " partaker in the tribulation and kingdom and endurance which are in Jesus," with the original apostolate. The editorial note, as it is often regarded, with which the Gospel closes, suggests the apostolic authorship. The First Epistle is entirely anonymous, whilst the Second and Third Epistles come from one who styles himself " the Elder."

In the third quarter of the second century the Johannine authorship of the Gospel and Apocalypse was accepted as the judgement of the Church. Since the researches of de Bruyne[1] and the further discussion by Harnack,[2] it has come to be widely accepted that the anti-Marcionite Prologues, as they are called, formed the first introduction to the collection of writings put forward as canonical in opposition to

---

[1] " Les plus anciens prologues latines des Évangiles," *Revue Bénédictine*, xl. 193–214 (July, 1928).

[2] *Die ältesten Evangelien-Prologe und die Bildung des NT* (1928).

the arbitrary canon of the heresiarch Marcion. The Lucan Prologue, which alone survives in its original Greek, closes with the sentence, " Afterwards John the Apostle, one of the Twelve, wrote the Apocalypse in the island of Patmos, and after that the Gospel." The Latin translation of the Johannine Prologue has come down to us in a variety of MSS., with a considerable amount of textual corruption. Amongst several statements of dubious value it is clearly stated that the Gospel of John was given to the churches by John during his lifetime, and that Papias records this in his five books of Expositions. Whatever may be the worth of these Prologues in matters of historical detail, they are at any rate sufficient to throw some discredit upon the attempts so persistently made to use the name of Papias to support the theory of the early martyrdom of the Apostle John. A few years later Irenaeus, in a number of passages too well known to be quoted here,[1] gives powerful support to the tradition that John the Apostle survived until the reign of Trajan and resided in Asia Minor. This is the kind of subject upon which such evidence is of considerable value. The literary question of authorship, however, stands in a different category, and it is here that internal evidence must be allowed to speak with preponderant authority. There are two witnesses who may be called at this point. Justin Martyr, whose *Dialogue with Trypho* took place in Ephesus about the year A.D. 136, attributes a quotation about the millenium to " a man among us named John, one of the Apostles of Christ," who " prophesied in a Revelation made to him."[2] In the *Apology*, written some years after that date,

---

[1] These passages are cited in W. F. H., *The Fourth Gospel*, p. 248.
[2] *Dial*. lxxxi. 4.

Justin shows his possible acquaintance with the Fourth Gospel by several loose quotations or echoes of its language,[1] but he nowhere cites it on the authority of John. A century after Justin, Dionysius, Bishop of Alexandria, in a discussion quoted at length by Eusebius,[2] gives reasons based upon both doctrinal conceptions and literary style, for assigning the Apocalypse to one author and the Gospel and Epistles to another. But whereas Justin assigns apostolic authorship to the Book of Revelation, Dionysius ascribes the Gospel and Epistles to John the Apostle and Beloved Disciple, and the Apocalypse to another John who lived and was buried at Ephesus.

The most searching examination of the linguistic peculiarities of the Apocalypse makes it almost impossible to think of it as coming from the author of the Gospel and Epistles. In subject-matter the difference is even more marked. But we must not lightly assume that there is no connection. Amongst those who dismiss the Son of Zebedee entirely from the Johannine literature, some of the most eminent commentators on the Apocalypse call attention to common features so striking as to suggest a common origin. W. Bousset, who wrote the best German commentary on Revelation, and R. H. Charles, whose two volumes in the International Critical Commentary are the most exhaustive treatment of the book in English, both recognize that, in spite of remarkable differences in style and contents which prove separate authorship, there are yet phrases and doctrinal similarities which point decidedly to some connection between the two authors. Charles goes so far as to say : "The Evangelist

---

[1] *Apol.* I. vi. 2 ; xxxvi. 6 ; lii. 12 ; lx. 3 ; lxi, 4, 5.
[2] *H.E.* VII. xxv.

was apparently at one time a disciple of the Seer, or they were members of the same religious circle in Ephesus." [1] Professor Lohmeyer, in his exposition of Revelation,[2] identifies the Seer with John the Presbyter, who may have written the Gospel in Aramaic in Syria, and some time afterwards the Apocalypse in Greek. Perhaps the most ingenious attempt to relate the various Johannine writings was that offered by Johannes Weiss.[3] According to this elaborate scheme John of Asia Minor in the later sixties wrote an Apocalypse, arising out of no contemporary events, in which he repeated the old predictions of the Lord. Later on he wrote his Epistles in opposition to those false teachers in whom he espied the Antichrist, thus paying tribute to the apocalyptic tendency of his time by recognizing the ancient prophecy of the Antichrist, and seeing its fulfilment in a definite portent. But, as his letters show, he had already outgrown it, and when he wrote down his recollections of his Lord, which became in his hand a preaching of the Incarnate Word, he had almost entirely laid aside eschatology ; he was no longer expecting the Lord ; the Messianic age when God would dwell among his people was already present, the life of the Lord was the long-hoped-for theophany. John had outlived all the eyewitnesses of the life of Jesus ; he had outlived, as it seemed, even his own work. When, in the reign of Domitian, the Church was plunged into deep distress he had neither the vigour nor the inclination to adapt his prophecy of the Church to the new situation. Another editor combined with his original apocalypse of thirty years

[1] *Op. cit.*, p. xxxiii.
[2] Lietzmann's *Handbuch zum NT*, IV. v. 199.
[3] *Die Offenbarung des Johannes* (1904), 162ff.

before a composite prophetic Jewish work written about the time of the fall of Jerusalem, and published the apocalypse thus edited in order to rally the churches of proconsular Asia to face a terrible crisis. John himself was an honoured survivor of the first Christian generation around whose name legends were gathering in his lifetime. The editor of his Gospel inserted the passages about the Beloved Disciple when he published it after his death. Thus, in course of time, the belief arose that the author was no other than the Son of Zebedee. This is an interesting attempt to bring into one coherent system the various writings that bear the name of John. It has, however, been accepted by few, if any, scholars. But Johannes Weiss made one significant remark. These writings all came from the same circle, in the same region of the Church, about the same time. They reckoned upon being accepted and understood by the same constituency. The inference to be drawn is that we must allow scope in the outlook of these churches for two points of view which to us seem almost irreconcilable, the apocalyptic and the immanental-mystical. In a later lecture this will call for special attention.

The position taken up in these lectures is that while all five books originated in the same circle the Apocalypse stands apart. Its grammatical idiosyncrasies point to separate authorship, and its employment of Jewish non-Christian sources involved the incorporation of conceptions which are distinct from the views that are characteristically Johannine. The Book of Revelation will therefore be left out of account, except for the occasional illustration of thoughts which are central to the teaching of the Gospel and Epistles.

The relation between the Evangelist and the writer

of the Epistles is by no means certain. The extra-ordinarily strong resemblance in vocabulary and style has convinced most scholars that they were written by the same author. The volumes in the International Critical Commentary by J. H. Bernard on the Gospel, by A. E. Brooke on the Epistles, and by R. H. Charles on Revelation all assemble a mass of linguistic evidence in favour of the view that the author of the Gospel also wrote the Epistles. But this must not be regarded as a *chose jugée*. Sixty years ago the greatest New Testament critic and expositor of his generation in Germany, H. J. Holtzmann,[1] after an exhaustive examination of the data, gave his judgement against the unity of authorship. That view was shared by Hans Windisch in his commentary on the Catholic Epistles, and, most important of all, Professor C. H. Dodd[2] has recently re-examined the question and given reasons for attributing the First Epistle to a devoted disciple of the Evangelist who had " soaked himself in the Gospel, assimilating its ideas and forming his style upon its model."

The problem is further complicated by theories of editorial revision. There can be little doubt that the Gospel underwent some adjustment and additions after the death of the Evangelist before it was given to the world. The theories of extensive redaction associated with the names of J. Wellhausen and B. W. Bacon[3] belong to an epoch when the analytic propensity was allowed to run riot. But the latest commentary on the Gospel, that by Professor Rudolf

---

[1] For references to Holtzmann and Windisch, see W. F. H., *The Fourth Gospel*, p. 257.

[2] *Bulletin of the John Rylands Library*, xxi. 1. pp. 129ff (April, 1937).

[3] See W. F. H., *The Fourth Gospel*, pp. 76ff. ; 111ff. ; 258.

Bultmann now appearing in Meyer's series,[1] seems in places to show a return to this subjective treatment by postulating an " ecclesiastical redaction," especially in the third and sixth chapters, where in the interests of sacramental tradition and usage the original form of the Gospel is supposed to have suffered considerable interpolations. Bultmann, however, is on much safer ground when he alludes to various sources used by the Evangelist. What these sources were is largely a matter of conjecture. Until recently it has been regarded as almost beyond doubt that both Mark and Luke were used by the writer of the Fourth Gospel. Dr. Gardner-Smith's investigations have led him to the startling conclusion that the Fourth Evangelist had not read any of the Synoptic Gospels, and that, like the other Evangelists, he drew upon the same store of Christian tradition.[2]

From the earliest days, traditions of the Lord's sayings and doings were current. Some of these, before long, became stereotyped in the official preaching and teaching of the Church. After a while, as we know from the preface to St. Luke's Gospel, much of this common tradition had been reduced to writing. The Fourth Evangelist has made free use of a variety of material at his disposal. He has put on it the stamp of his own mind. With the exception of a few passages [3]

---

[1] *Kritisch-exegetischer Kommentar über das Neue Testament.* Das Johannes-Evangelium (1937–   ).

[2] *St. John and the Synoptic Gospels* (1938). With one proviso, I am almost persuaded by the cumulative weight of the arguments. The qualification which I should make is, that before the Gospel was published there was some verbal assimilation to a few of the Marcan and Lucan narratives (such as the Anointing, and the Feeding of the Multitude) by the hand of the Editor.

[3] *E.g.* xiii. 1–4.

a unity of style marks the writing throughout the Gospel. We recognize the same style to a considerable extent in the Epistles. But here a difference is to be expected. The Gospel was probably the slow growth of many years of preaching, teaching, meditation, and reflection. It deals throughout with the sublime theme of the Incarnate Son of God and the revelation of the divine glory by means of a life passed under conditions of time and space. It was manifestly left by the author in a state which made a certain disarrangement of the papyrus sheets possible, if not inevitable, thus offering some opportunity for editorial comments and connecting links.[1] The Epistles, on the contrary, were more hurried productions, applying the main thoughts of the Gospel to the practical needs of the churches which looked up to the aged disciple as a Father in God. He may have followed the practice of St. Paul in dictating his letters, and it is possible that he left his amanuensis a certain freedom of expression. One factor ought never to be overlooked. Such a pastoral treatise as the First Epistle of John was written under the stress of an urgent need to deal with a situation which had arisen in a group of churches. The peril seemed grave to the venerable leader. In such a mood the language of eschatology emerges to meet the crisis that threatens the whole church with disaster.[2]

Johannine Christianity is but one aspect of the

---

[1] See W. F. H., *The Fourth Gospel*, pp. 125–41, 264.

[2] In the judgement of the writer, the Gospel and the Epistles were written or dictated by the same venerable leader of the Church in proconsular Asia. The Gospel represents his meditations and teaching over a number of years and was *published* after his death. The Epistles were written near the end of his life to those who were familiar with the teaching embodied in the Gospel.

common Christianity of the primitive Church. Its teaching is the most highly developed in the New Testament, but behind all the theological interpretation we can discern the outline of the apostolic preaching, and beneath the whole structure of faith we can trace the foundations of the evangelic history of Jesus of Nazareth. The main facts of the ministry of Jesus as told by the earliest Christian preachers are laid down in the Johannine Gospel. Journeying from Nazareth and known as the Son of Joseph, Jesus came south to the valley of the Jordan where John was baptizing. Though the actual baptism of Jesus is not recorded (probably for polemical reasons), yet the Baptist's contrast between his own baptism administered by water and the future baptism by his Successor with holy spirit is associated with the sign of the Spirit's descent in the form of a dove. The call of the disciples, who are later referred to as the Twelve, miracles of healing, disputes with Jewish rigorists about a cure on the sabbath day, which led to a further charge against him of blasphemy, the feeding of the multitude followed by a midnight meeting with the distressed disciples in such fashion as to deepen their sense of awe, waxing and waning popularity with the Galilean crowd, Peter's confession on behalf of the Twelve, the enmity of the religious leaders in Jerusalem, the treachery of Judas, the last supper, the arrest in the garden, the ineffectual armed resistance, the trial before the High Priest, the charge before Pilate, the condemnation and crucifixion, followed by appearances of the Risen Lord—all this belongs to the primitive tradition, with whatever variations in detail, arrangement, and emphasis. Most remarkable is the disproportionate amount of space devoted, as in the other

Gospels, to the last week in Jerusalem. But this no longer seems out of scale when we remember that the one Gospel, according to whatever Evangelist, was fundamentally the preaching of the Cross. This is attested in St. Paul's memorable words, " Now I make known unto you the gospel which I preached unto you, which ye also received, wherein ye also stand, by which also ye are saved. . . . For I delivered unto you first of all that Christ died for our sins according to the scriptures ; and that he was buried ; and that he hath been raised on the third day according to the scriptures ; and that he appeared to Cephas ; then to the Twelve," and so on.[1]

The Fourth Gospel, together with its earliest commentary, the First Epistle of St. John, might seem to have been written to fit that description of apostolic preaching. The word " gospel " indeed is not used, but its Johannine equivalent is " witness." That witness was delivered, it was to be received ; those who received it were to abide in the truth to which it testified, that they might be saved, or, in Johannine phrase, might have eternal life. But that is not all. The twice-repeated " according to the scriptures " in the Pauline outline of the gospel emphasizes the earliest method of appeal to divine authority in the preaching which claimed Jesus as Messiah. This was the appeal to the scriptures. Now, if we find fewer Old Testament references in St. John than in St. Matthew, " we must also observe," as Dr. Rendel Harris reminded us, " that when they do occur they betray acquaintance quite clearly with the method and the contents of the primitive Testimony Book," [2]

---

[1] 1 Cor. xv. 1ff.   [2] *Testimonies*, Part II, p. 71.

or so-called Messianic proof-texts from the Old Testament. However far-fetched some of these quotations may seem to the modern mind, and whatever violence they are often felt to do to sound exegesis, the method was one familiar and acceptable to the Jewish mind. It also paid homage to the accepted view that the divine action in this world is pre-determined and does not depend upon the chances and changes of human effort. All through this Gospel we seem to hear the striking hours, telling us that the time is not yet, or that it is drawing near, or that the hour has come for the fateful decision and the decisive act. But it carries the conception still further in recognizing the symbolism of the day and the hour of the crucifixion. The Son of God was crucified at the very time when the paschal lamb was being slain in the Temple. As such it was in accordance with scripture that " not a bone should be broken." [1] From first to last, in the Johannine outlook, it must have been clear to discerning eyes, that, as Philip said, " We have found him of whom Moses in the law, and the prophets did write," and as Nathanael affirmed, " Thou art the Son of God ; thou art King of Israel." [2] Thus the avowed purpose of the Gospel is expressed in words that comply with the pattern of the Pauline κήρυγμα, " These things are written that ye may believe that Jesus is the Christ, the Son of God, and that believing ye may have life in his name." [3]

This bold assertion reminds us that we must not expect to find in the Fourth Evangelist a detached spectator of events, or a disinterested chronicler of the sayings and doings of Jesus. The differences between

[1] John xix. 36 ; cf. Exod. xii. 46, Num. ix. 12. [2] John i. 45, 49.
[3] John xx. 31.

the Synoptic Gospels and St. John have been pointed out so often that they need not be elaborated here. As our present interest is rather with the Johannine presentation of Christianity than with discussions about the relative historicity of divergent records, we may limit our attention to three methods of theological emphasis which mark the Johannine narrative. They may be called for convenience, *explicative* emphasis, *mandatory* emphasis, and *proleptic* emphasis.

(*a*) The first method is that of unfolding to the eye of the reader some feature in the ministry of our Lord which was known to the primitive tradition ; where, however, it was not conspicuous, but was indicated by some shadowy saying or vague allusion. There are few passages in St. Mark which have caused more perplexity and discussion than the statement attributed to Jesus about his use of the parabolic method of teaching (Mark iv. 10–14). It is generally agreed that the words as here recorded cannot have been spoken by Jesus. The difficulty was evidently felt by the later Synoptists. It is incredible that Jesus spoke in parables to create unbelief. Moreover Professor C. H. Dodd [1] has shown that the vocabulary of these verses belongs to a later stage of thought than that of the ministry in Palestine. Most writers are inclined to credit St. Mark with an application of the Pauline πώρωσις apologetic [2] from Romans to the Galilean situation. Ever since Jülicher's *magnum opus* [3] opened a new chapter in the exegesis of the Parables it has been almost a common-

---

[1] *The Parables of the Kingdom*, pp. 13f.

[2] *I.e.* the theory in Rom. xi. 7–10, illustrated from Isa. xxix. 10, Deut. xxix. 4, and Ps. lxix. 22–5, that a spirit of insensibility smote the rest of Israel whilst those who exercised the discernment of faith inherited the promises.

[3] *Die Gleichnisreden Jesu* (1888–99).

place that every parable was a clear illustration of a
single theme and nothing more. But there have not
been wanting scholars who see in the persistence of this
quotation from Isaiah vi. 9–10 in all the Synoptics
an evidence that Jesus did say something that pointed
to a profounder purpose in some of his parables. The
most thorough-going and successful treatment of this
difficult passage is that which Professor T. W. Manson
has offered.[1] By retranslating the Targum of Isaiah and
recognizing the ambiguity of the Aramaic particle
which corresponds at the same time to the Greek
relative pronoun and to the final particle, he recon-
structs the probable words of Jesus after this fashion :
" But all things come in parables to those outside who
see indeed but do not know, and hear indeed but do
not understand, lest they should repent and receive
forgiveness." According to this interpretation, the
" Sower " is a parable about parabolic teaching. The
theme is the character not of the seed but of the
different kinds of soil. In Dr. Manson's words, " the
quotation from Isaiah is not introduced by Jesus to
explain the purpose of teaching in parables, but to
illustrate what is meant by οἱ ἔξω : it is in fact a
definition of the sort of character which prevents a
man from becoming one of those to whom the secret
of the kingdom is given, a description in language
borrowed from the Jewish Bible of those people who
did not produce the things for which Jesus was continually seeking—insight, repentance, and faith."

Forty years ago, in the first volume of the *Journal of
Theological Studies*, Dr. Sanday wrote a long review
of Jülicher's famous book. He deprecated the facile
assumption that Jesus spoke no word about the sifting

[1] *The Teaching of Jesus*, pp. 75ff.

effect of his teaching. " In St. John's Gospel . . . our Lord speaks of His own preaching as of itself, by a sort of automatic process, dividing between believers and unbelievers. . . . It was but a working out of the prophecy of Simeon, ' Behold, this child is set up for the falling and rising of many in Israel ' (Luke ii. 34). The whole ministry had this effect, but we might regard it as culminating in the Parables." [1] Let us examine this parallel more closely. In St. John we have no parables but the acted parables of the signs (σημεῖα), by which word he prefers to describe the mighty works of Christ. St. John also quotes this famous text from Isaiah, after another favourite Testimony from the song of the Suffering Servant. " These things spake Jesus, and he departed and hid himself from them. But though he had done so many signs before them, yet they believed not on him : that the word of Isaiah the Prophet might be fulfilled which he spake . . ." [2] With St. John, however, this is not enough. The theme is first heard in the Prologue : " He came to his own place, and his own people did not receive him. But to as many as received him he gave the right to become children of God, even to those who believe on his name." [3] It becomes a recurring refrain throughout the Gospel ; thus, " For judgement did I come into the world that those who see not may see ; and that those who see may become blind." And when some Pharisees asked in return, " Are we also blind ? " Jesus replied, " If you were blind, you would have no sin ; but now you say, We see : your sin remains." [4] This is the Gospel of the Crisis ; the Gospel of the Rejection.

[1] *J.T.S.* i. p. 176. [2] John xii. 36f. [3] John i. 11f.
[4] John ix. 38–41.

(b) The second method, that of *mandatory emphasis*, crystallizes in a phrase a conception of Jesus which is found in solution in the earlier tradition, and by constant repetition applies it as a title to Jesus. At the very beginning of the ministry in the Marcan record Jesus says to his disciples, " Let us go elsewhere into the next towns, that I may preach there also ; for to this end came I forth," [1] which St. Luke rightly interprets, " for to this end was I sent." [2] For the sermon at Nazareth, but a short time before, was preached from the text containing the words, " He hath *sent* me to proclaim release to the captives." [3] Yet the conception that the ministry of Jesus is a message from God is not prominent in the Synoptic Gospels. It finds its most characteristic expression in the saying common to all three, " Whoever receives me receives him that sent me." [4] This saying is also preserved by St. John, who is not satisfied, however, with a merely incidental reference. In his Gospel the phrase ὁ πέμψας με, " He who sent me," is found on the lips of Jesus no less than twenty-six times, whilst the verb ἀποστέλλω (used by John with precisely the same meaning) occurs eighteen times in the Gospel for the Son's mission from the Father, and three times in the First Epistle. The term " He who sent me " is in this Gospel a divine title, and when the *Auctor ad Hebraeos* called Jesus " the Apostle of our confession," [5] he expressed in one noun what St. John proclaims in a verbal phrase on almost every page. It sums up all the

---

[1] Mark i. 38, εἰς τοῦτο γὰρ ἐξῆλθον.

[2] Luke iv. 43, ὅτι ἐπὶ τοῦτο ἀπεστάλην.

[3] Luke iv. 18.

[4] Mark ix. 37, Matt. x. 40, xviii. 5, Luke ix. 48, x. 16, John xii. 44, xiii. 20.

[5] Heb. iii. 1, τὸν ἀπόστολον τῆς ὁμολογίας ἡμῶν.

prerogatives and functions of prophecy in the unique mission of Him who came from the bosom of the Father to reveal the nature of Him whom no man has seen.

(c) The third method, that of *proleptic emphasis*, is that Johannine characteristic by which the end is seen from the beginning, so that instead of a gradual self-disclosure, the revelation in its fullness is proclaimed by anticipation from the opening of the ministry. Two illustrations of this may be offered in the contrast between the Marcan and the Johannine treatment of (i) the Messianic Secret, and (ii) the Transfiguration.

(i) Even the most casual reader can see that in St. John the Messianic Secret is an open secret from the beginning. Before we have finished the first chapter it is being shouted from the house-tops. John the Baptist has proclaimed Jesus as the Son of God (or, as an important variant reading has it, " the Chosen One of God "), and as the Lamb of God who takes away the sin of the world. Andrew has discovered in Jesus the Messiah, Philip is reporting that he has found one in whom all Old Testament prophecy is fulfilled, and Nathanael has hailed Jesus as Son of God and King of Israel. To crown all this convergent testimony, Jesus himself in unmistakable language has claimed the title, Son of Man. Nevertheless this is an anticipatory representation of truth. It is programmatic. But beneath the surface there is far more in common with the Christian tradition than at first appears.

Julius Schniewind, in his admirable commentary on St. Mark,[1] makes the Messianic Secret the key to the understanding of the Gospel, whilst putting the term to a very different use from that of its coiner, Wilhelm

[1] *Das Neue Testament Deutsch*, i. 1 (1937).

Wrede.[1] In a note at the close of the first chapter of Mark, after referring to the repeated injunctions that the healed should preserve silence about the worker of their cure, Schniewind writes, " This feature is part of the ' Messianic Secret' of Jesus. Already, while on earth, Jesus is the king appointed by God, but in secret, in concealment. W. Wrede, who was the first to take notice of the Messianic Secret, regarded all these features as later additions to the portrait of Jesus. But it will appear that this secret underlies every narrative and every saying of Jesus in our Gospels. Jesus never works his miracles as a magician ; he shuns success (John vi. 15ff., vii. 33ff.) ; he refuses every demand for a sign (Mark viii. 11ff., John vi. 30ff., iv. 48). It is of a piece with this that Jesus performs his miracles, even the greatest of them, solely as one who prays for them (John vi. 23, ix. 31, xi. 41ff.), as one who receives from the Father, and that he completely disavows all display of the miracle, entirely repudiating the rôle of miracle-monger. The miracles are ' signs,' for they point beyond themselves to the sovereignty of God." [2]

(ii) Still more obvious is the contrast between the Synoptic story of the Transfiguration and that which we find as its anticipation and substitute in the Johannine Prologue. " And we beheld his glory, glory as of an only-begotten [3] from the Father, full of grace and truth. . . . No man has seen God at any time. The divine One, the only Son, who is in the bosom of the Father, he has declared him." This glory shines

---

[1] *Das Messiasgeheimnis in den Evangelien* (1901).   [2] *Op. cit.* p. 54.

[3] For the meaning of μονογενής see p. 69. This rendering of the phrase μονογενής θεός is given by Dr. Moffatt as a necessary periphrasis, without accepting the variant reading υἱός for θεός.

forth from Jesus throughout his life, and no mention is made anywhere of that supreme occasion when " he received from God the Father honour and glory, when there came such a voice to him from the excellent glory, This is my beloved Son in whom I am well-pleased." [1]

But we miss the deep significance of the Johannine method if we overlook two things. First, the Transfiguration story in the Synoptic tradition is closely related to Peter's confession and to the subsequent interpretation of Messiahship in the light of the Suffering Servant. Now, whilst in St. John the words δόξα and δοξάζειν are used a few times of the divine glory revealed in the life of Jesus, they are used far more in the second half of the Gospel when "the crisis of this 'glorification' is the Passion consummated in the Risen Life." [2]

The second point is one that has been brought out by Lohmeyer in a striking excursus on the Transfiguration in his commentary on St. Mark.[3] After drawing attention to the eschatological significance of the title Son of Man borne by Jesus in the Marcan account, he continues : "It shows the Son of Man, not in his function as Judge of the world, as the visions in Daniel describe him, but as One with whom Moses and Elijah speak, that is as One whose existence is of import only to the one people chosen of God. And this definition is of a peculiar kind. He is not saving, not sanctifying and glorifying the people. He is teaching three disciples who hearken to his word. If Mark elsewhere speaks of the healing and exorcising ministry, and places preaching in the background, here speaking

[1] 2 Pet. i. 17.

[2] J. H. Bernard, *I.C.C.* St. John, i. p. 22.

[3] *Krit.-exeg. Kommentar über das NT.* Das Ev. des Markus, p. 179.

and speech are the only instrument of this Son of Man, and his only efficacy. We have therefore a Johannine touch in this story. That which in John is implicit throughout the story of Jesus from beginning to end : μονογενὴς θεὸς . . . ἐκεῖνος ἐξηγήσατο (i. 18, cf. Peter's confession, vi. 68) is here shown once for all in this event and in the command accompanying it, ἀκούετε αὐτοῦ, 'hear ye him.' " [1]

Johannine Christianity, according to ancient tradition, had its centre and first home in proconsular Asia. It is therefore natural to ask how far it was influenced by its intellectual and religious environment. Greek philosophy has sometimes been regarded as a factor, and this was due to the prominence given to the Logos in the Prologue. There is nothing else in the Gospel or Epistles to encourage such a theory. A far more plausible case was made out for Philonic influence. There are many striking coincidences of thought, but the differences are so fundamental that anything but a slight and indirect contact is improbable.

Within the last generation attempts have been made to affiliate Johannine ideas to Hellenistic mystery religions,[2] to Mandaean gnosticism,[3] and to the

[1] According to Lohmeyer, one of the most significant features of the Transfiguration is the revelation of the divine δόξα in the One who speaks for and from God—his Logos, in fact.

[2] Thus, W. Bousset (Kyrios Christos [2], pp. 163ff.) explained John vi. 40 and 1 John iii. 2 by " deification through the vision of God," an idea common in the Hellenistic piety of the mystery religions, and without any true parallel in O.T. religion. Prof. A. D. Nock (" Early Gentile Christianity," in Essays on the Trinity and the Incarnation, pp. 106f.), emphasizes the difference from Hellenistic " God-mysticism." " The first Johannine passage does not postulate an immediate transformation : the fruit of vision is in eternal life. The second also looks to the Parousia or Second Coming."

[3] See W. F. H., The Fourth Gospel, pp. 24f., 91ff., 95, 171, 173. Also L.Q.R., January 1927.

peculiar form of syncretistic Hellenism found in the Hermetic writings. The most that can be said is that, in commending Christianity to the surrounding pagan world, terms belonging to the religious vocabulary current in these regions were sometimes borrowed. Indeed, there can be little doubt that Hellenistic Judaism from the time when it spoke Greek and read its scriptures in a translation instead of in Hebrew, was unconsciously but increasingly becoming acclimatized in the world of Hellenism. But the more closely the Johannine writings are studied the more clearly does the Jewish character of both language and thought stand out.[1]

This Judaic temperament would perhaps never have been overlooked but for the varying attitudes which the writer appears to take up towards the Jewish religion, with its sacred writings and institutions. On the one hand the Evangelist seems to regard the Jews indiscriminately with veiled hostility. He reproaches them with their ignorance of God and their failure to accept his Messenger. Christ is viewed as the perfect revelation of God, so that his predecessors in the history of revelation are of no account. Even the sacred Torah is eclipsed by the fresh revelation in Jesus Christ, whose new command has entirely replaced Jewish legalism. On the other hand, as we have seen already,[2] Scripture is appealed to in the form of Messianic testimonies. Abraham and Moses have foreseen the Christ or borne witness to him. The scribes are blamed not for their diligent searching of the scriptures but for their failure to see the wood for the trees and to discern the path that led through them to Christ. Old Testament types are found in

---

[1] See Additional Notes, A and B.   [2] See pp. 20, 24.

the serpent lifted up in the wilderness, and in the
manna given from heaven. The Scripture cannot be
broken. Salvation is of the Jews.[1]

Here we may find a partial parallel to the dual
attitude of St. Paul to Judaism. Paul has never been
forgiven by his own race for his trenchant criticism of
Pharisaic legalism. Yet he was a Jewish patriot with
an unquenchable pride in the religious traditions of
his race, and an undying gratitude for his moral
discipline in the Law. When he had won emancipation
from the bondage of Mosaic legalism he could still
write with perfect sincerity : " The law is holy, and the
commandment holy and righteous and good." [2] To
the end he was a Jew in all the deepest workings of his
mind. The Fourth Evangelist was a Jew in training
and tradition. But he could not forget that his people
had rejected the Messiah, and he had found such
complete satisfaction in the life of communion with the
Lord Jesus that the Synagogue no longer made any
appeal to him. In the following lectures, however, we
shall see again and again that the clue to the main
Johannine conceptions is to be sought in Jewish sources
rather than in foreign cults and philosophies.[3]

One thing remains to be said before we pass from
these preliminary observations. No interpretation of
Johannine thought is possible which leaves out of
account two factors. First, a deep and intense personal
devotion to Jesus Christ lies behind these writings.
They are not a collection of scraps gathered from
numerous writers who were interested in theoretical
views and contemporary discussions. There is one
master mind behind the Johannine writings, and he

---

[1] John viii. 56, v. 46, v. 39, iii. 14, vi. 32, 50f., 58, x. 35, iv. 22.
[2] Rom. vii. 12.   [3] See, e.g. pp. 45ff., 109ff., 124f., 196.

was a devoted disciple, whatever his name may have been. Secondly, he was no solitary thinker, however commanding his spiritual authority. The title which was given to one of the finest expositions [1] of the Johannine Epistles describes also the circle in which his meditations on the Jesus of history and the Christ of experience were thought out until they took shape in the Gospel : " Fellowship in the Life Eternal."

In the following lectures we shall try to trace some of the leading ideas in the Johannine theology. First comes the term Logos, which confronts us in the exordium of both Gospel and Epistle. Though in itself a word borrowed from the vocabulary of Greek philosophy, we shall show that it represents ideas which are rooted in the Old Testament, and must be interpreted in the light of the Gospel story of a human life which, in perfect filial trust and obedience, revealed the character and purpose of God. This leads on to the teaching about God—Father, Son, and Holy Spirit, developing and clarifying conceptions which seem to have been present in the Christian tradition from the beginning, though further elaborated in the preaching of St. Paul. We have then to consider human nature and its need of the divine revelation given in Jesus Christ. If salvation by revelation is at first sight the Johannine emphasis in contrast to the Pauline gospel of salvation by redemption, we must not ignore the presence in St. John's Gospel and Epistles of passages which show that the writer shared the common Christian belief in the reality of sin and of judgement, and of Christ's mission to cleanse from sin and to save men from perdition into fullness of life. Inasmuch as Johannine Christianity is set in the framework of the

[1] By G. G. Findlay (1909).

original apostolic preaching, its Judaic eschatology is in the background of thought throughout. Yet the mystical element, present in some of the recorded sayings of Jesus and brought into prominence in the Pauline teaching, reaches its climax in the Gospel and First Epistle of St. John. One of the most difficult tasks for the interpreter is to reconcile these two elements, Eschatology and Mysticism. Another paradox is presented by the teaching about the Church, the Ministry, and the Sacraments. No group of churches at the close of the first century could be indifferent to the disciplined life of the Christian community, nor to the interpretations to which its sacramental life so readily lent itself in the world of Hellenism. This is no doubt the reason why those writings which set forth so richly the interior life of personal devotion have so much to say about the outward means of grace. Ecclesiasticism is absent, but not the Church. Nevertheless the Christian religion is a personal relationship, and for St. John, as for every teacher who breathed in that world an atmosphere impregnated with gnosticism, the burning question is, "How can we know God?" Faith, Knowledge, and Love are closely related in the Christian apprehension of God, and the Johannine use of these terms demands close study. Finally, we shall end as we began, on the note of Revelation. Man's quest for God is anticipated and met in God's gift to man. Jesus, the Word, the Messenger, the Son, is the Way, the Truth, and the Life.

CHAPTER II

THE LOGOS OF LIFE

THERE is a scene in a once-famous novel by Mr. H. G. Wells [1] which describes a curiously assorted gathering in a large drawing-room when with startling suddenness the question was put: "Why, Bishop, was the Spermaticos Logos identified with the Second and not the Third Person of the Trinity?" That question sounds strangely out of place in such a company in this country in the twentieth century. But the λόγος σπερματικός (or Seminal Reason) was a term widely used in the centuries immediately before and after the beginning of the Christian era, and its meaning would have been understood at once in any company of educated men in Athens or Alexandria or Ephesus, at the end of the first century.

Indeed it was in this very city of Ephesus, some six centuries before that date, that Heraclitus first made use of the Logos idea, that is, the divine reason, immanent in nature and in man. "He seems to conceive it," writes James Adam,[2] "as the rational principle, power, or being which *speaks* to men both from without and from within—the universal Word which for those who have ears to hear is audible both in nature and in their own hearts, the voice, in short, of the divine." And again: "In Heraclitus the three conceptions,

---

[1] *The Soul of a Bishop.*   [2] *The Religious Teachers of Greece*, p. 222.

Jesus never works his miracles as a

magician — he shows successes.

to others

Ln VI. 15ff. ∼II 33ff.

I/who everything for 8yn.   II/h VIII.   le P 27.

The miracles are signs for the spirit. beyond

Themselves 6 the concept of God. !!

10.425 - 74
10.397.81
10.086.7

Logos, Fire and God, are fundamentally the same. Regarded as the *Logos*, God is the omnipresent Wisdom by which all things are steered." [1]

The Stoics followed with their conception of the primordial source of all things, the ethereal Fire. This Fire, eternal and divine, is endowed with creative activity. " The orderly working of Nature was its operation : organic beings grew according to regular types, because the Divine Reason was in them as a λόγος σπερματικός, a *formula* of life developing from a germ " (in the words of Dr. Edwyn Bevan).[2] In the course of time this theoretical pantheism attained a religious warmth, as in the noble *Hymn to Zeus* of Cleanthes or in the Discourses of Epictetus.

Not long after the Fourth Gospel made its way into the world, Justin Martyr, still wearing his philosopher's cloak, became, as Eusebius [3] puts it, an ambassador of the Divine Logos in the guise of a philosopher. He seized upon the term *Logos*, whether he had read this Gospel or merely heard sentences quoted from it in the current phraseology of the Ephesian church. He then developed his theory of the λόγος σπερματικός that every man at birth shares in the universal reason. But since Christ is the incarnation of the *Logos* in its entirety, " those who have lived with reason (μετὰ λόγου), even though they were reckoned atheists, are Christians, such as among the Greeks Socrates, Heraclitus, and those like them." [4] No doubt the daring theory which Justin propounded had much to do with the belief that St. John's Gospel is based upon a Greek philosophical speculation. But it is Justin rather than John who is responsible for the misunderstanding.

[1] *The Religious Teachers of Greece*, p. 233.   [2] *Stoics and Sceptics*, p. 43.
[3] *H.E.* IV. vi. 8.   [4] *Apol.* I. xlvi. 3.

Dr. Bevan has acutely remarked : " It is sometimes said that the Stoic σπερματικὸς λόγος was parallel to the cosmic *Logos* of Philo or the Fourth Gospel, but in the fragments of the old Stoic books the word is habitually used in the plural, σπερματικοὶ λόγοι, for the multitude of specific types reproduced by propagation. Stoicism knew of no cosmic *Logos* distinct from God or the Divine Fire : where they speak of the λόγος of the world in the singular they generally mean the ' scheme ' of the world." [1]

If it may be said that the Stoics had brought the term *Logos* from the Porch into the street before the spread of Christianity into the Gentile world, we must also acknowledge that at the very time that the new faith rose upon the world a Hellenistic Jew was carrying it from the study to the Synagogue. This was Philo of Alexandria, a son of Israel, whose native tongue was Greek, whose bible was the Septuagint, and whose intellectual home was Athens. Alexandria had been for long the active centre of Hellenistic culture, with a large and influential Jewish population which lived in strained and restless rivalry with their Gentile neighbours. It was in this city that the Seventy had wrought their legendary miracle of conveying the infallible Law into an inspired translation. It was here that Ben-Sira's Hebrew book of Wisdom was turned by his grandson into Greek, and that a successor enriched the Wisdom Literature of Later Judaism with a noble work in which a Greek mind sought concealment behind the mask of Solomon. The fusion of Greek thought and Hebrew religion found its consummation in the numerous writings of Philo.

This prolific writer uses the word *Logos* no fewer than

[1] *Later Greek Religion*, p. xv.

thirteen hundred times, with such a bewildering variety of meanings that it is only possible now to quote a few passages where he refers to the divine *Logos*. " The primal existence is God, and next to him is the Logos of God." [1] Again, " The image of God is the Logos, through whom the whole universe was framed."[2] Or, " Who then can the House be, save the Logos who is antecedent to all that has come into existence ? the Logos, which the Helmsman of the Universe grasps as a rudder to guide all things on their course ? Even as, when he was fashioning the world, he employed it as his instrument, that the fabric of his handiwork might be without reproach." [3] In another passage he likens the Universe with all that it contains to a flock under the hand of God its King and Shepherd. " This hallowed flock he leads in accordance with right and law, setting over it his true Logos and Firstborn Son who shall take upon him its government like some viceroy of a great king." [4] Again, " If the whole creation . . . is a copy of the divine image, it is manifest that the archetypal seal also, which we aver to be the world descried by the mind ($\kappa\acute{o}\sigma\mu o s$ $\nu o\eta\tau\acute{o}s$), would be the very Logos of God." [5] To the same effect he writes elsewhere, " When the substance of the Universe was without shape and figure God gave it these ; when it had no definite character God moulded it into definiteness, and when he had perfected it, sealed the universe with an image and idea, even his own Logos." [6] The latest editors of Philo [7] have suggested that Logos, here and elsewhere, is the image ($\epsilon\grave{\iota}\kappa\acute{\omega}\nu$) of God, and the ideal form ($\grave{\iota}\delta\acute{\epsilon}a$) to

---

[1] *Leg. All.* ii. 86. [2] *Spec. Leg.* i. 81. [3] *Migr. Abr.* 6.
[4] *Agr.* 51. [5] *Op. Mund.* 25. [6] *Somn.* ii. 45.
[7] F. H. Colson and G. H. Whitaker in the Loeb *Philo*, vol. v. p. 607.

creation. This may be said to correspond to the use which Philo makes in several passages of the old Stoic distinction between the λόγος ἐνδιάθετος, the Logos inherent in God, and the λόγος προφορικός, the Logos emanating from God, *e.g.* " As in each of us, Reason has two forms, the outward of utterance and the inward of thought." [1]   Whatever Philo owed to the Academy and to the Porch,[2] he was also influenced by Jewish speculation, as when he identifies this semi-hypostatized conception with Wisdom. In a characteristically allegorical description of the Garden of Eden he writes, " ' River ' is generic virtue, goodness. This issues forth out of Eden, the wisdom of God, and that is the Logos of God." [3]

To sum up in the briefest possible way, Philo uses the term Logos to express the conception of a mediator between the transcendent God and the universe, an immanent power active in creation and revelation, but though the Logos is often personified, it is never truly personalized.

There was, however, another source of religious speculation which may have carried this word Logos into regions where Christians mingled with Hellenistic Jews and became acquainted with the language of mystical syncretism. Much attention has been given in recent years to an obscure stream which in the early centuries of the Christian era contributed to the general

---

[1] *Vit. Mos.* ii. 129. οὐ μὴν ἀλλὰ καὶ δυσὶ λόγοις τοῖς καθ' ἕκαστον ἡμῶν, τῷ τε προφορικῷ καὶ ἐνδιαθέτῳ, δύο ἀρετὰς ἀπένειμεν οἰκείας, τῷ μὲν προφορικῷ δήλωσιν, τῷ δὲ κατὰ διάνοιαν ἀλήθειαν.

[2] For Philo's debt to Plato and the Stoics see Zeller, *Die Philosophie der Griechen in ihrer geschichtlichen Entwicklung* [3], III. ii. pp. 360ff., and much more briefly in *Grundriss der griechischen Philosophie*, ed.[12] (Leipzig, 1920), pp. 346ff. (E.T. by L. R. Palmer (London, 1931), pp. 259ff.)

[3] *Leg. All.* i. 65.

movement of religious thought called Gnosticism. It
is known as the Hermetic writings. Everyone is
familiar with those lines in *Il Penseroso* where Milton
sings :

> Or let my lamp at midnight hour
> Be seen in some high lonely tower,
> Where I may oft outwatch the Bear
> With thrice-great Hermes, or unsphere
> The spirit of Plato, to unfold
> What worlds or what vast regions hold
> The immortal mind, that hath forsook
> Her mansion in this fleshly nook :
> And of those demons that are found
> In fire, air, flood, or under ground,
> Whose power hath a true consent
> With planet or with element.

But few indeed are those who have ever in these days
troubled to look into the remains of that large body
of astrological and magical writings which were
attributed to a deified sage who taught in Egypt in
a remote past. He was the Egyptian god Thoth, often
called in their language " very great, great," who was
identified with the Greek god Hermes. Quite distinct
from this pseudo-science was another type of writing,
in which religious speculation and philosophical
instruction assumed the form of discourses of Hermes
Trismegistus, just as the apocalyptic writers of later
Judaism sought sanction for their works by publishing
them as revelations written by ancient seers. Soon
after the dawn of the Renaissance a manuscript was
brought from Macedonia to Italy, containing a number
of tractates which professed in most cases to be discourses by Hermes Trismegistus. Numerous editions
were printed before the close of the fifteenth century.

In course of time this interesting literature was almost
forgotten, but early in this century the labours of
Richard Reitzenstein in Germany rescued it from
oblivion, and his work was popularized in this country
by the enthusiastic service of the late Mr. G. R. S.
Mead, whose translation was published under the title
Thrice Greatest Hermes. Then in the twenties the
Oxford University Press brought out the standard
edition of the *Hermetica* in four volumes, representing
the life-work of the English scholar Walter Scott, who
thus claimed for this type of speculative and de-
votional mysticism a new place in the field of com-
parative religious studies. Of the eighteen tractates in
the Corpus Hermeticum some are as late as the third
century of our era, and it is doubtful whether any can
be dated as early as the first century. But they are
valuable as showing a kind of religious interest, originating outside Judaism, which blended Greek philosophical ideas with material suggested by some contact with
the Septuagint and with Hellenistic Jewish mysticism.
The first of these *libelli* bears the name *Poimandres*.
Here the cosmogony of Genesis has provided a foundation for speculative theories in which the Logos idea
plays a prominent part. As there seems to be here no
sign of direct contact with Christianity, Professor
C. H. Dodd, who has devoted special study to this
literature, shows that the parallels between the Poimandres and the New Testament can be best explained " as the result of minds working under the same
general influences." [1] Therein he reaches the same
conclusion as Dr. Estlin Carpenter, who wrote :
" With some common religious terminology, and corresponding appeals to analogous phases of inner

---

[1] *The Bible and the Greeks*, p. 247.

experience, the Hermetica and the Fourth Gospel appear wholly independent. Each makes its contribution to the spiritual life of its age in its own form. Each seeks the knowledge of God, and each finds it in a communion opened to the soul from the divine side by an act of grace. The Greek mystic realizes it through Nature, the Christian through Christ." [1]

"In the beginning was the Logos, and the Logos was with God, and the Logos was divine." [2] Thus the Fourth Gospel begins. "That which was from the beginning, that which we have heard, that which we have seen with our eyes, and our hands have handled, concerning the Logos of life." So the First Epistle of John opens. We have seen that the term was not new, but was in widest use both in religious and philosophical discussions about the relation of God to his world both of nature and of man. But in no writings outside the New Testament is there any true parallel to the statements made about the Logos in the Johannine Prologue. Yet this doctrine was no novelty in the teaching of the Church. The surprising thing is that the term is found in a personal sense in these two passages alone in the entire New Testament, apart from the title "Word of God" in the description of the conquering hero in the Apocalypse. [3] This is the more surprising in that the Logos doctrine is present in all but name in several passages in the Pauline Epistles. It finds its fullest expression in the Christological argument in the first chapter of Colossians, but it is already present in

[1] *The Johannine Writings*, p. 312.
[2] For a discussion of the predicative use of θεός in this verse see *The Letters of Principal James Denney to W. Robertson Nicoll*, pp. 124f.
[3] Rev. xix. 13.

B2

1 Corinthians. " It was an easy matter," writes Canon Wilfred Knox,[1] " for Paul in writing his first letter to Corinth to transfer the person of the historical Jesus from the category of the heavenly Messiah of Palestinian Judaism and Christianity into that of the divine Wisdom which was the centre of Hellenistic Jewish speculation, where the term Logos had not yet ousted it under the influence of Philo." But surely in Paul's time the term must have been known in Ephesus, especially when we remember that at that very time there had come to Ephesus a certain Jew named Apollos, an Alexandrian by race, who was mighty in the scriptures, to whom Priscilla and Aquila expounded the way of God more perfectly. However, Mr. Knox writes in a footnote : " It is interesting to observe as showing the gradual diffusion of language in the synagogues of the Dispersion that Paul is not acquainted with Philo's far more convenient word, while the author of the Fourth Gospel is. The latter writer has even less contact with Philo's outlook than Paul himself, but Philo's term has become by this time a commonplace of the synagogues."

There may be another reason, for Paul is not the only Christian writer of that period to resist the almost invincible pressure of the inevitable word. The *Auctor ad Hebraeos*, who, if not Apollos, must have been, spiritually speaking, his twin brother, or at farthest remove his first cousin, reveals in every page the influence of the Alexandrian school of Old Testament exegesis. He seems, in the resounding exordium of his discourse, to challenge his readers to hail their Lord as ὁ Λόγος τοῦ Θεοῦ. " God having of old time spoken

[1] *St. Paul and the Church of the Gentiles*, p. 114.

unto the fathers in the prophets by divers portions and in divers manners, hath at the end of these days spoken unto us in a Son, whom he appointed heir of all things, through whom also he made the worlds ; who, being the effulgence of his glory, and the very image of his substance, and upholding all things by the word of his power, when he had made purification of sins, sat down on the right hand of the Majesty on high." [1]

There must have been some reason which led both Paul himself and also the anonymous Alexandrian to avoid a word which would have clinched their argument with their cultured contemporaries. There is some internal evidence that an inhibition was imposed upon the use of the closely related term Wisdom. In 1 Corinthians Paul boldly proclaimed, " But of him are ye in Christ Jesus, who was made unto us Wisdom from God, even righteousness and sanctification and redemption." [2] But in his later letters he never repeats the title. Even in Colossians, where his language is evidently chosen from the vocabulary of the Wisdom books and he writes of Christ as the " image of the invisible God, the first-born of all creation," [3] he does not make the expected declaration that Christ and Wisdom are one. But with a side glance at the shibboleths of Gnosticism he does say that in Christ " all the treasures of knowledge and wisdom are hidden." [4] Equally significant is the way in which the author of *Hebrews* never uses the word Wisdom in his discourse, though in the opening verses no reader can fail to

[1] Heb. i. 1–3.   [2] 1 Cor. i. 30.

[3] Col. i. 15 : $\epsilon i \kappa \grave{\omega} \nu \ \tau o \hat{v} \ \theta \epsilon o \hat{v} \ \tau o \hat{v} \ \dot{a} o \rho \dot{a} \tau o v, \ \pi \rho \omega \tau \dot{o} \tau o \kappa o \varsigma \ \pi \dot{a} \sigma \eta \varsigma \ \kappa \tau \dot{\iota} \sigma \epsilon \omega \varsigma.$

[4] Col. ii. 3 : $\dot{\epsilon} \nu \ \hat{\wp} \ \epsilon i \sigma \iota \nu \ \pi \dot{a} \nu \tau \epsilon \varsigma \ o \dot{\iota} \ \theta \eta \sigma a v \rho o \dot{\iota} \ \tau \hat{\eta} \varsigma \ \sigma o \phi \dot{\iota} a \varsigma \ \kappa a \dot{\iota} \ \gamma \nu \dot{\omega} \sigma \epsilon \omega \varsigma \ \dot{a} \pi \dot{o} \kappa \rho v \phi o \iota.$

recognize echoes of the famous description of Σοφία
in the seventh chapter of the Wisdom of Solomon.[1]

> For she is a breath of the power of God,
> And a clear effluence of the glory of the Almighty ;
> Therefore can nothing defiled find entrance into her.
> For she is an effulgence from everlasting light,
> And an unspotted mirror of the working of God,
> And an image of his goodness.

The similarity of thought is impressive, but the use, in
both, of the word ἀπαύγασμα (effulgence) settles the
question of literary dependence beyond dispute.

It has often been observed that St. John avoids the
use of the words Γνῶσις (knowledge), Πίστις (faith), and
Σοφία (wisdom), and it is generally accepted that his
reason lies in their appropriation as sectarian watch-
words by certain Gnostics. Were Γνῶσις and Σοφία
already beginning to be so used at the time of Paul's
later letters and when the Epistle to the Hebrews was
being written ? It may well be that the term Logos
had already been appropriated as a catchword of
some Jewish or semi-Christian sect.

This leads us to the point at which we must examine
the use of the term by St. John. It occurs in the
Prologue to the Gospel and in the preface to the Epistle.
This use is as appropriate as its absence henceforth is
significant.

The Prologue to the Gospel has every appearance of
being a summary prefixed after the Gospel had been
written. But is it an original composition by the
Evangelist ? Twenty years ago Professor V. H. Stanton
gave reasons which need not be rehearsed for the
opinion " that in the Prologue and the remainder of

---

[1] Wisd. vii. 25f.

the Gospel we have the history of the evangelist's thought in inverse order." [1] How then did he come to place this term in the forefront of his Gospel ? The answer to this question in all probability may be supplied as the result of three converging lines of evidence. First came the argument by Dr. Rendel Harris [2] that behind the Prologue lay a hymn in honour of Wisdom, which in its turn depends on the eighth chapter of Proverbs. It would be an easy transition in Greek-speaking circles to substitute a masculine noun for a feminine one, as the Wisdom-doctrine and the Logos-doctrine were closely akin. Then came Dr. C. F. Burney's book, *The Aramaic Origin of the Fourth Gospel*.[3] Whatever may be thought of the success or failure of the attempt to prove that the whole Gospel has been translated from an Aramaic original, or that in many cases the Greek text is due to mistranslation of this original Aramaic, a *prima facie* case has been made out for the poetic structure of the Prologue. A retroversion into Aramaic reveals " the form of a hymn, written in eleven parallel couplets, with comments introduced here and there by the writer." [4] Finally, Professor Rudolf Bultmann, in an essay contributed to Gunkel's *Festschrift*,[5] made the suggestion which he repeats in his new commentary on the Fourth Gospel, that the Evangelist incorporated, with additions of his own, a hymn that originated with the sect that honoured John the Baptist.

Literary structure and the interrupted sequence of thought both argue for the theory that editorial revision has taken place at some stage in the history of the Prologue. But everything points to an adaptation

---

[1] *The Gospels as Historical Documents*, iii. p. 178.
[2] *The Origin of the Prologue to St. John's Gospel* (1917). [3] (1922).
[4] *Op. cit.* p. 40. [5] ΕΥΧΑΡΙΣΤΗΡΙΟΝ, ii. pp. 1–26.

of a poem previously composed.[1] By common consent
verses 6–8 are an intrusion into the original poem, and
there are other traces in the Gospel of a polemic, not
against John but against those who exalted him at the
expense of the Greater One who followed him. Burney
would include in this polemical gloss verses 9 and 10,
also 15, and would find interpretative glosses in verses
12–13, 16b and 18. Bultmann limits the glosses to
verses 6–8, 15 and 17, those, that is, which refer to the
Baptist, together with the clause contrasting law and
grace, and a few short insertions. He therefore
assumes that the sect of John the Baptist accepted
all for their master that the Evangelist claimed for
Jesus Christ. But he recognizes that verses 14, 16, 18
may also be additions of the Evangelist and he suspects
that the words " Jesus Christ " in 17, as in xvii. 3, have
been added. These clauses are of the very essence
of the Christian message, and the bold assertion of the
incarnation of the Logos outstrips all that Gnostic
and Philonic speculation had reached. There is
strong reason to believe, therefore, that the Fourth
Evangelist has taken over a hymn about the Logos,
based as it was upon speculation about the Heavenly
Wisdom, and has amplified it at several points to
remove it from its former application or misinterpreta-
tion and to bring it into closest agreement with the
marvel of the earthly life of him whom the Church

[1] The theory that the Prologue is an adaptation of an earlier hymn
does not mean that the Christology is borrowed. What Prof. A. D.
Nock writes of the status of St. John Baptist among the Mandaeans
applies equally to the germ-cell of Mandaism, the Baptist sect of the
first century : " This view of John arose in opposition and rivalry to
the Christian view of Jesus, and is not prior or independent." *Essays
on the Trinity and the Incarnation* (edited by A. E. J. Rawlinson), p. 98,
n.[3].

had come to recognize as divine. The Prologue as it stands is now an integral part of the Gospel. It matters not from what source it originally came. It has been baptized into Christ. What then does the word Logos mean to the Evangelist ? In what sense is the Prologue an introduction to the rest of the Gospel, and how is it related to the message of the First Epistle ?

The Gospel must not be interpreted by the term Logos, rather must we understand this term with its varied history in the light of the Gospel as a whole. The Prologue in its present form has been accepted and adapted by the Evangelist. The overwhelmingly Jewish tone and setting of the Gospel reminds us that the Evangelist uses the term in a way that accords with Jewish ideas. There are three lines of thought which meet.

(a) The opening sentence of the Prologue inevitably recalls the opening sentence of Genesis, when the creative word called the universe into being.[1] In innumerable passages in the Old Testament the Word of the Lord is used to describe either the exercise of the divine power, or the revelation of the divine character, will, or purpose.

> By the word of the Lord were the heavens made ;
> And all the host of them by the breath of his mouth.
> For he spake, and it was done ;
> He commanded, and it stood fast.[2]

Or again, " So shall my word be that goeth forth out of my mouth : it shall not return unto me void, but

---

[1] The resemblance is unaffected by the rendering of Gen. i. 1–3, demanded by the syntax of these verses. See Skinner, Genesis, *I.C.C.* p. 13. Ecclus. xliii. 26, " By his word all things consist " reads differently in the Hebrew.

[2] Ps. xxxiii. 6, 9.

it shall accomplish that which I please, and it shall prosper in the thing whereto I sent it." [1]   It has often been assumed that this conception was developed in later Palestinian Judaism into a personification represented by the Aramaic word *Mēmrā*. But the Hebrew word *Dābhār* is never so rendered in the Targums. *Mēmrā* is never employed to express either the dynamic word of creation or the medium of revelation. Billerbeck has shown in his exhaustive examination [2] of the term and its uses, and his results are sustained by G. F. Moore, [3] that *Mēmrā* is not an intermediary nor a hypostasis, but only a purely formal substitute for the sacred tetragrammaton, the ineffable name. It is therefore the Old Testament rather than the Targums that led some distance towards the special use of Logos.

(*b*) Reference has already been made more than once to the influence of the Wisdom literature upon the development of the Philonic doctrine of the Logos. The starting-point is the eighth chapter of Proverbs, where the figure of Wisdom is the speaker.

> The Lord possessed me in the beginning of his way,
>   Before his works of old.
> I was set up from everlasting, from the beginning,
>   Or ever the earth was. . . .
> When he established the heavens, I was there : . . .
>
> When he marked out the foundations of the earth :
> Then I was by him, as a master workman :
> And I was daily his delight,
> Rejoicing always before him ;
> Rejoicing in his habitable earth. [4]

[1] Isa. lv. 11.

[2] *Kommentar zum NT aus Talmud und Midrasch*, ii. pp. 302–333.

[3] *Judaism*, i. pp. 417ff. Moore's emphatic judgement is that *Mēmrā* is purely a phenomenon of translation, not a figment of speculation ; it never gets outside the Targums. *Ib.* p. 419.   [4] Prov. viii. 22ff.

Speaking of the works of the Creation, Ben Sira writes : "By the word of God are his works," [1] and Pseudo-Solomon writes :

> O God of the fathers and Lord who keepest thy mercy,
> Who madest all things by thy word ;
> And by wisdom thou formedst man.[2]

(c) But there was a third direction in which the way was prepared for the Johannine use of the term Logos. In the Wisdom of Ben Sira we first meet with the identification of Wisdom with the Torah. At first this becomes evident by the exchange of terms in parallel clauses. Thus, after speaking of the search for Wisdom, the writer says :

> For he that feareth the Lord doeth this ;
> And he that taketh hold of the Law findeth her (i.e. Wisdom).[3]

Again :

> Without deceit shall the Law be fulfilled,
> And Wisdom is perfect in a mouth that is faithful.[4]

Again :

> He that keepeth the Law controlleth his natural tendency,
> And the fear of the Lord is the consummation of Wisdom.[5]

But in two later chapters the identification is made more certain :

> All wisdom is the fear of the Lord,
> And all wisdom is the fulfilling of the Law.[6]

[1] Ecclus. xlii. 15.
[2] Wisd. ix. 1, 2. See Oesterley, *Introduction to Books of Apocrypha*, p. 116, and footnote.
[3] Ecclus. xv. 1. [4] *Ib*. xxxiv. 8. [5] *Ib*. xxi. 11. [6] *Ib*. xix. 20.

The most decisive passage is in Chapter XXIV, which devotes twenty-two verses to a panegyric of Wisdom, and then abruptly declares :

All these things are the book of the covenant of the Most
    High,
The Law which Moses commanded as an heritage for the
    assemblies of Jacob.[1]

This identification of the Torah with Wisdom [2] involved as a corollary not only the divine character but also the pre-existence of the Law, and is evidence that this doctrine was accepted long before the Christian era. The word Torah, which means " instruction," stood for more than a code of commandments. C. G. Montefiore [3] described it as the " middle term between Israel and God." It was the object of intense devotion to the pious Jew. Dr. Peake [4] writes of the " prolix enthusiasm " for the Torah shown by the author of the 119th Psalm. But in rabbinic Judaism we find statements about the Torah which supply astonishing parallels to the Johannine Prologue. The following points deserve attention. Corresponding to the words " *In the beginning*," pre-existence is ascribed to the Torah. Thus, " Seven things were created before the world was created ; namely, the Torah, Repentance, the Garden of Eden, Gehenna, the Throne of glory, the Temple, the Name of Messiah." " *The Logos was with God*." Compare with this : (The Torah) " lay on God's bosom, while God sat on the throne of the glory."

---

[1] Ecclus. xxiv. 23. See Oesterley in *Apocrypha and Pseudepigrapha of O.T.*, i. pp. 305f.

[2] On this identification see further, W. L. Knox, *St. Paul and the Church of the Gentiles*, pp. 57, 60, 62, 69.

[3] *Peake's Commentary*, p. 620.

[4] *The Servant of Yahweh and Other Lectures*, p. 242.

" *The Logos was divine.*" So we read : " My daughter, she is the Torah." " *All things were made through him.*" Note the parallel : "Through the first-born God created the heaven and the earth, and the first-born is no other than the Torah." " *In him was life.*" Even so : "The words of the Torah are life for the world." "*And the life was the light of men.*" So in 2 (4) Esdras, xiv. 21 : " for the world is set in darkness, and they that dwell therein are without light, for thy Torah is burnt, therefore no man knoweth the things that are done of thee, or the works that shall be done." " *Full of truth.*" In the Midrash on the Psalms we find : " Truth, by this the Torah is meant."

Such examples, which are taken from Billerbeck's commentary [1] and from Kittel's article in his Theological Dictionary, [2] are enough to raise a presumption that the Evangelist knew that the hymn which he adopted was written in praise of Wisdom, in her later aspect as the Torah. But there is a further indication of this. We have already observed that there are comments introduced into the text of the hymn to guard against a misapplication to a historical figure whose followers set him in rivalry against Jesus. But there is one unmistakable gloss to point the superiority of the New Torah over the old. " The Torah came by Moses. Grace and truth came by Jesus Christ." Is there not a further contrast ? When Moses was to go up to the holy mount to receive the tables of stone, he asked : " Show me, I pray thee, thy glory." And the Lord replied : " Thou canst not see my face : for man shall not see me and live." [3] When the new Torah was given, it is written : " No man hath seen God at any

[1] *Op. cit.* ii. pp. 353, 355, 357, 361 ; iii. p. 131.
[2] *Theol. Wörterb. z. NT.*, iv. p. 139.　　　[3] Exod. xxx. 18, 20.

time. God, the only-begotten, who is in the bosom of the Father, he hath interpreted." [1]

Two words in this Prologue stand out for their sacred Jewish associations. Δόξα is the Hebrew *Kābhōdh*, the Aramaic *Y'qārā* of the Targums. Ἐσκήνωσεν inevitably recalls the Hebrew *Sh'kīnā*, the Aramaic *Sh'kīntā*. Burney [2] gives several examples of the use of these terms in the Targums, or Aramaic paraphrases of the Old Testament. Thus Exod. xxv. 8 : " That I may dwell in your midst," becomes " That I may cause my *Sh'kīntā* to dwell among you " ; and Isaiah lvii. 17, " I hid myself," becomes " I caused my *Sh'kīntā* to depart (ascend) from them." In the same way, Exod. iii. 6: " For he was afraid to look upon God," becomes, " For he was afraid to look upon the manifestation of the *Y'qārā* of the God of Israel," and Exod. xxiv. 10, " And they saw the God of Israel," becomes, " And they saw the *Y'qārā* of the God of Israel." The Torah had become the symbol and pledge of the divine presence with his people. But it had its stern side, and it was given " on Sinai's height, in cloud and majesty and awe." " And so fearful was the appearance that Moses said, I exceedingly fear and quake." [3] Of the old Torah it is said " it *was given*," of the new Torah that " grace and truth *came* through Jesus Christ." In three verses the writer harps upon this aspect of *gracious* reality. Never once throughout the rest of the Gospel is that word " grace " used. In spite of its dominating use in the Pauline

---

[1] For Moffatt's rendering of John i. 18, see p. 27, n.[3]. Büchsel (*Theol. Wörterb.*, ii. p. 910) would translate ἐξηγήσατο " revealed."

[2] *Aramaic Origin of Fourth Gospel*, pp. 35f. See also R. D. Middleton, " Logos and Shekinah in the F.G.", *Jewish Quarterly Review*, N.S. xxix, pp. 101ff. (Oct. 1938).   [3] Heb. xii. 21.

vocabulary of salvation, John restricts his use to the closing verses of the Prologue. It is the climax of his announcement of the Gospel. Henceforth the story itself will set forth this Figure of ineffable grace and glory.

Λόγος and Νόμος, Word and Torah, are now identified. But what more lies behind this emphasis upon Λόγος at the very beginning of the story ? There is the divine imperative in the teaching of Jesus. The Sermon on the Mount contains the claim to reinforce and to reinterpret the Law of Sinai, and to go far beyond. In that teaching there was more than command ; there was revelation of the character of God. But the life itself was a revelation, not least in the death and the resurrection. So the early Church regarded that life in its entirety as the word which God had spoken when he visited and redeemed his people. The first disciples were " those who from the beginning had been eye-witnesses and ministers of the Word." [1] The Gospel, the message brought by Jesus Christ and proclaimed about him, was the " word of the cross," the " word of reconciliation," the " word of truth," the " word of life." [2] When Paul said to the Jews at Pisidian Antioch : " To us was the word of this salvation sent forth," [3] he was speaking of the Gospel, but as a word spoken by God and sent forth by God in a personal life. And when he commended the Ephesian elders at Miletus " to God and to the word of his grace," [4] he was using an expression which can be paralleled in many other parts of the New Testament ; all of which goes to show that the early Church thought

[1] Luke i. 2.
[2] 1 Cor. i. 18 ; 2 Cor. v. 19 ; Eph. ii. 13 ; Phil. ii. 16.
[3] Acts xiii. 26.   [4] Acts xx. 32.

of its message as an expression of an act and word of God spoken to the world in a living and historic revelation.

This brings us to the opening words of the First Epistle. We are no longer concerned with pre-Christian speculations about Wisdom or Law. They have made their contribution to the vocabulary of Christian thought. Here we have to do with the Christian way of life, with the new commandment, with the divine authority of the revelation upon which the life of the Christian community depends. The emphasis is now altogether upon the qualifying genitive, " the Logos *of life*." The memorable words of the Prologue to the Gospel find their echoes in phrases which link the present message with the historic revelation, and set the revealing word in its true relation to the eternal past. In Jesus Christ we are in touch with reality, with the very nature of God himself. The testimony of the Church guarantees the reality of the message as one founded upon a life in which men saw the glory of God, and found the grace of the divine Fatherhood through fellowship with him who revealed the perfect trust of true Sonship. The emphasis is changed according to the needs of those who are being addressed, and it has well been said that : " it is the fourth verse rather than the first of the Gospel which supplies the text for the Epistle " ; [1] " in him was life, and the life was the light of men." That life will be shared with the members of the redeemed community according to their response in righteousness, faith, and love.[2]

" It is of what existed from the very beginning, of

---

[1] G. G. Findlay, *Fellowship in the Life Eternal*, p. 86.
[2] Robert Law, *The Tests of Life*, pp. 5f.

what we heard, of what we saw, of what we witnessed and touched with our own hands, it is of the Logos of Life (the Life has appeared ; we saw it, we testify to it, we bring you word of that eternal Life which existed with the Father and was disclosed to us)—it is of what we heard and saw that we bring you word, so that you may share our fellowship ; and our fellowship is with the Father and with his Son Jesus Christ. We are writing this to you that our own joy may be complete." [1]

The reiterated emphasis upon the reality of the Lord's human life points to a prevalent danger. Some docetic heresy such as that of Cerinthus, who taught that Christ, a divine being, descended upon Jesus at the Baptism and left him before the Passion, may be in the writer's mind. [2] A hazy intellectualism, some variety of Gnosticism which relied upon esoteric knowledge of God and disparaged the vulgar interest in the Gospel story, may have constituted the immediate peril. The reply is clear and uncompromising. There is One and only One through whom eternal life is given to men. He was with the Father from the beginning ; his earthly life made visible to men the Life which existed with the Father. This Life has now become an experience of men enjoying fellowship with the Father and the Son, who is none other than Jesus Christ. In the prologue to the Gospel the Logos is finally announced as the only begotten Son who reveals the glory of the Father. In the preface to the Epistle the Logos is defined as the Son who imparts

---

[1] 1 John i. 1–4 (Moffatt). Westcott, supported by A. E. Brooke, interprets ὁ λόγος τῆς ζωῆς, " the revelation of life." For the other view, which takes ὁ λόγος as in the prologue to the Gospel, see R. Law, *ib*. pp. 44f., 370.   [2] *Cf.* 1 John ii. 22ff.

the life of fellowship with the Father. The uniqueness of this relationship is implied by the avoidance of the word " sons " for Christians, who are " children of God." [1] It is asserted again and again : " This is the testimony, that God gave us eternal life, and this life is in his Son. He who has the Son has the life ; he who has not the Son has not the life." [2] " No one who denies the Son has the Father ; he who confesses the Son has the Father also." [3] " We know that the Son of God is come, and has given us an understanding to know him that is true, and we are in him that is true, even in his Son Jesus Christ. This is the true God and eternal life." [4] The final statement of the message concerning the Logos of Life is reached in the salutation of the Second Epistle : " Grace, mercy, peace shall be with us from God the Father, and from Jesus Christ, the Son of the Father, in truth and love." [5]

---

[1] Unlike St. Paul, St. John never uses υἱὸς θεοῦ of any but Christ. We are τέκνα θεοῦ.

[2] 1 John v. 11f.   [3] 1 John ii. 23.
[4] 1 John v. 20.   [5] 2 John 3.

CHAPTER III

FATHER, SON, AND HOLY SPIRIT

ONE of the best-known chapters in his *Confessions* [1] is that in which St. Augustine tells how in the Platonic books he found the divinity of the Eternal Word, but not the humility of the Incarnate Word. In a Latin translation of some neo-Platonic writings he discovered in all but verbal identity much that is written in the opening verses of the Johannine Gospel. But there were two passages in that Prologue to which he could find no parallel. He looked in vain elsewhere for such words as: "He came unto his own, and his own received him not, but as many as received him to them he gave the right to become children of God, even to those who believe on his name." Then he declares: "But that 'the Word became flesh and dwelt among us,' this I found not there."

St. Augustine is not the only one to find that the Fourth Evangelist is concerned not with a speculative philosophy, but with a Gospel of recorded fact. He does indeed make tremendous affirmations about the nature and purpose of God, but they are all based upon the revelation contained in the human life of Jesus. In the words of a recent German writer: "All theological utterances in John are at the same time Christo-

[1] Bk. VII. chap. ix.

logical. The perfect and the present always presuppose the aorist." [1]   This is specially noticeable in the Gospel where the story of the earthly life of the Son is the medium through which the Father is revealed. In the First Epistle, God as the source of the teaching of Jesus is brought more directly into the forefront of the message.   Dr. Estlin Carpenter, [2] following H. J. Holtzmann, [3] has pointed out how significant is the difference in the appellations which are used. Whereas in the Gospel the Father is mentioned one hundred and nineteen times, and is called God seventy-nine times, in the First Epistle there is quite a different ratio, for the name Father is only given twelve times, whilst the word God is used sixty-four times. It is unnecessary to accentuate the difference, which is due not to divergent conceptions, but to the modes of expression suitable to the occasion and purpose of each writing. When the Evangelist attempts to compress into a sentence the meaning of " eternal life," that *summum bonum* of all religion, he defines it as continuous progress in knowledge of " the only true God, and him whom thou hast sent, Jesus Christ." [4]   The same thought appears in the Epistle as " Our fellowship is with the Father and with his Son, Jesus Christ." [5]   Needless to say, when the Gospel was presented to the Gentile world the sublime majesty of the Hebrew conception of the true God was assumed. " For thus saith the high and lofty One that inhabiteth eternity, whose

[1] Walther von Loewenich (of Erlangen), *Johanneisches Denken*, p. 17. In other words, a historic event had abiding results, and profoundly affects our present apprehension of God.

[2] *The Johannine Writings*, p. 345.

[3] *Lehrbuch der Nt. Theologie*, ii. p. 444.

[4] John xvii. 3.   The present stem of the verb $\gamma\iota\nu\acute{\omega}\sigma\kappa\omega$ is used.

[5] 1 John i. 3.

name is holy." [1] This ethical conception of God,
which was the great legacy of the Hebrew prophets,
is represented in the Gospel by one simple but significant sign. In the prayer of Chapter XVII, where the
perfect trust of the Son in the Father finds its com-
pletest expression, twice over in direct appeal the most
sacred title of confident intimacy is qualified by an
adjective : " Holy Father," " Righteous Father." [2]
Nowhere else in the New Testament is that noun so
qualified, though we may say that this is implicit in
the Matthaean form of the Lord's Prayer.[3] Again, in
the First Epistle, " He is righteous " [4] recalls us more
than once to this fundamental aspect of the divine
character. But there runs through the Old Testament
the thought of God as " the living God," [5] the Creator
of heaven and earth, and the giver of life to all men.
Hebrew thought was concerned with the conception
of the Divine nature not as abstract being, but as the
source of active forces operative in the world. The
creative activity of God is not prominent in the Johannine writings. The pre-existent Logos in the Prologue
represents this divine agency. But there is one interesting passage in the Gospel in which Jewish speculation on this theme comes to light.

In reply to a charge of Sabbath-breaking brought
against him after the healing of the infirm man at
Bethesda, Jesus defended his action with the words :
" My Father worketh even until now, and I work." [6]
The point of that reply is that contemporary Jewish

---

[1] Isa. lvii. 15.   [2] John xvii. 11, 25.   [3] Matt. vi. 9.
[4] 1 John ii. 29 ; iii. 7.
[5] This phrase occurs ten times in the O.T. : Deut. v. 26, Joshua iii.
10, 1 Sam. xvii. 36, 2 Kings xix. 4, 16 (=Isa. xxxvii. 4, 17), Ps. xlii. 2.
lxxxiv. 2, Jer. x. 10, xxiii. 36, Hosea i. 10. For the rich content of this
title see Sanday, *Inspiration*, pp. 124ff.   [6] John, v. 17.

thought attributed continuous activity to God, but of an ethical kind. In the *Letter of Aristeas* the story is told that when King Ptolemy asked one of the Seventy, " Wherein does piety consist ? " the answer was wisely given, " In the belief that God is working in and has knowledge of all things at all times, and that no unrighteous deed or evil action of man can escape his eye ; for as God is benefactor of the whole world, so wouldst thou, by imitating him be void of offence." [1] The Rabbis were hampered in their thought of continuous divine activity by texts in the Pentateuch which record the Sabbath rest of God. [2] They solved their problem by discriminating between God's work as Creator and as Judge. God rests from physical work on the Sabbath, but is continually active from the beginning to eternity in works of judgement. These comprise both the condemnation of the wicked and the conferment of life. [3]

Three great affirmations about the essential nature of God stand out in the Johannine writings. But on closer examination we see that they are intended to declare not so much what God is in his essential being as what in that character he communicates to men, and what he requires of those who come to him in worship, or to enjoy fellowship with him.

GOD IS SPIRIT. [4] This is no new revelation. It is common to Jewish and Greek thought. Solomon's dedicatory prayer avowed : " Heaven and the heaven of heavens cannot contain thee ; how much less this house that I have builded ! " [5]   The condition of com-

---

[1] *Ep. Arist.* 210.   [2] Gen. ii. 2 ; Exod. xx. 11 ; xxxi. 17.
[3] Odeberg, *The Fourth Gospel*, pp. 201ff. ; Billerbeck, *op. cit.* ii. pp. 461f. ; Bultmann, Commentary *in loc.*
[4] John iv. 24.   [5] I Kings viii. 27.

munion with God is that the highest that is in man, his πνεῦμα—"the likest God within the soul"[1]— should be in harmony with God, who is Spirit, and that his worship should be founded on the reality of the God whom he approaches. Yet the initiative is with God, who *seeks* such worshippers, and himself bestows the Spirit of truth.

GOD IS LIGHT.[2] This is one of several passages in the Epistle which Professor C. H. Dodd[3] is inclined to attribute to current Hellenistic thought. He quotes several passages from the *Hermetica* and from Philo. Two of these are impressive parallels. Thus Poimandres interprets to the seer a vision of unbounded light in the words: "That light am I, Reason, thy God."[4] Philo also writes, "First God is light, for there is a verse in one of the Psalms, 'the Lord is my illumination and my Saviour (κύριος γὰρ φωτισμός μου καὶ σωτήρ μου).' And he is not only light, but the archetype of every other light, nay, more ancient and higher than every archetype. For the pattern was the Logos which contained all his fullness—light, in fact ; for as the lawgiver tells us, God said, ' Let light come into being,' whereas he himself resembles none of the things which have come into being."[5]

The Philonic quotation is the more striking because of the further parallel to the statement in the Prologue about the Logos. "In him was life, and the life was the light of men. That which lightens every man coming into the world was the true light."[6] It may

---

[1] Tennyson, *In Memoriam*, liv. [2] 1 John i. 5.

[3] *Ryl. Libr. Bull.* xxi. (1937), p. 149.

[4] *Corp. Herm.* i. 6. (See W. Scott, *op. cit.* i. pp. 116f. for a different reading and rendering.) [5] *Somn.* i. 75.

[6] John i. 4, 9 (or, "The true light, which lightens every man, was coming into the world ").

be that the writer of the Epistle is consciously appropriating a term in current use among the Gnostics whom he is combating. Philo's reference to the twenty-sixth Psalm [1] is a reminder of the widespread use in Hebrew scripture of light as the self-communicating goodness of God, and of the conflict between light and darkness for the contrast between good and evil.

In the present context the ethical emphasis is unmistakable. The message received from Jesus—not necessarily crystallized into any *logion*, but the proclamation of the whole life of Him who called himself " the light of the world,"—is that " God is light, and in him is no darkness at all." [2] Christian fellowship is only possible for those who walk in the light. The profession of fellowship with God by those who walk in darkness is a manifest lie. Just as worship of God is only possible to those whose spirits are " in truth," so fellowship with God is unattainable by those whose actions are not " in truth."

GOD IS LOVE. [3] The crowning revelation made in Jesus Christ is that God is love. Here, once more and above all, we observe that what God is in his essential nature is set forth in terms of divine action. " Herein was the love of God manifested in us, that God hath sent his only-begotten Son into the world that we might live through him." [4] Nowhere is the close relationship of the First Epistle to the Gospel more clearly shown than in these words. " The gospel within the gospel," as Luther called John iii. 16, is the outstanding example of the theological value of grammar. It was surely of set purpose that St. John wrote, οὕτως ἠγάπησεν ὁ Θεὸς τὸν κόσμον, ὥστε τὸν Υἱὸν

---

[1] Ps. xxvi. (LXX), Ps. xxvii. (Heb. and E.V.).
[2] John viii. 12 ; 1 John i. 5.   [3] 1 John iv. 8.   [4] 1 John iv. 9.

τὸν μονογενῆ ἔδωκεν. He might have written ὥστε δοῦναι (" as to give ") to mark the measure of the potential gift. Instead, he writes, ὥστε ἔδωκεν (" that he gave") to declare the magnitude of the recorded act. Again we are confronted by the Divine initiative : " Herein is love, not that we loved God, but that he loved us and sent his Son " to remove the barrier erected by our sins.[1] " We love because he first loved us." [2] Yet again we note the ethical demand that accompanies the revelation of the Divine nature. " If God so loved us, we also ought to love one another." [3] Moreover, the love of God cannot abide in him who loves only in word or with the tongue. The practice of love is the condition of continuance in the family of God. Just as fellowship with God who is Spirit depends upon sincerity and reality in worship, and fellowship with God who is Light involves the practice of the truth, so fellowship with God who is Love is only attained by those who love " in deed and truth." [4]

" That God is Love," writes H. J. Holtzmann, " is both the highest enhancement of the Synoptic teaching of the Fatherhood of God, and the profoundest exposition of the spiritual nature of God. For it is just by this that the conception of God is entirely removed from the category of substance and finally taken out of the sphere of natural religion." [5] Others had taught that God is Spirit. Contemporary theosophies declared that God is Light. It was for Christianity, and especially St. John, to tell the world a higher truth, without which religion may not rise above metaphysics, or may sink into mythology.

---

[1] 1 John iv. 10. For the meaning of ἱλασμός, see the next lecture, pp. 98f.　　[2] 1 John iv. 19.　　[3] 1 John iv. 11.　　[4] 1 John iii. 18.
[5] *Lehrbuch d. Nt. Theologie*, ii. p. 443.

> " For the loving worm within its clod
> Were diviner than a loveless god
> Amid his worlds, I will dare to say." [1]

On a simple tombstone in the graveyard of Whatley in Somersetshire, marking the last resting-place of the greatest of the Deans of St. Paul's are engraved two stanzas from the most solemn and sonorous of the hymns of the Middle Ages, the *Dies Irae*.

> Rex tremendae majestatis,
> Qui salvandos salvas gratis,
> Salva me, fons pietatis.

> Quaerens me sedisti lassus,
> Redemisti crucem passus,
> Tantus labor non sit cassus.

Taken thus out of their original setting in the awe-inspiring scenery of the day of doom, these words bring together the two contrasted aspects of the portrait of Jesus which merge so marvellously in the Gospel according to St. John. How strangely do those haunting verses of Thomas of Celano carry us back to the Fourth rather than to the other three Gospels !

> King of majesty tremendous,
> Who dost free salvation send us,
> Fount of pity, then befriend us !

> Think, good Jesus, my salvation
> Caused Thy wondrous incarnation ;
> Leave me not to reprobation.

> Faint and weary Thou hast sought me,
> On the cross of suffering bought me ;
> Shall such grace be vainly brought me ?

[1] R. Browning, " Christmas Eve," v. (*Poetical Works*, i. p. 483).

And if we turn back to the preceding stanza, it is the First Epistle of St. John that leaps to the memory.

> What shall I frail man be pleading,
> Who for me be interceding,
> When the just are mercy needing?

Only in the Epistle to the Hebrews do we find the like blending of the royal dignity of the Son of God with the tender sympathy of the truly human Jesus who is touched with the feeling of our infirmities.[1] He who looks beneath the surface or reads between the lines of St. Mark will find the same contrast, but the total impression is not so startling. The "tremendous majesty" of the Johannine Christ is seen not so much in evangelic comments, such as that "He knew what was in man,"[2] or by the intensified magnitude of the "signs," as in the admiration which disarmed the temple police sent by the chief priests and the Pharisees,[3] or the awe which fell upon the band of soldiers and police in the garden when he whom they were to arrest exclaimed, "I am he."[4] It is seen in the prisoner's bearing before Pilate ; " My kingdom is not of this world." [5] But we recognize it most of all in the sublime confidence with which, on the night of his betrayal, after warning his disciples of all that lay ahead, he exclaimed : " But be of good cheer ; I have overcome the world." [6] It was this that kindled the answering faith that breaks out in the battle-cry of the believing Church in the First Epistle : " This is the victory that hath overcome the world, our faith. And who is he that overcometh the world, but he that

---

[1] Heb. i. 1–4, iv. 15. [2] John ii. 25. [3] John vii. 32, 46.
[4] John xviii. 6. [5] John xviii. 36. [6] John xvi. 33.

C

believeth that Jesus is the Son of God ? "[1]   Yet Docetism was only too ready to submerge the true humanity of Jesus in his divine splendour, and against this deadly peril readers of the Gospel are clearly warned in the declaration, " The Logos became flesh."[2]   The Evangelist does not shrink from recording the weariness and thirst of the Traveller who rests by the well at Sychar,[3] or the shuddering horror and the tears at the tomb of Lazarus,[4] or the cry from the cross, " I thirst."[5]   These are general impressions left upon the mind of every reader by the dramatic genius of the author.   There are, however, several points at which a closer investigation is needed.

It is strange that in a Gospel which lays so great a stress upon the divine origin of our Lord, and clearly teaches his pre-existence, not a word should be written about the mode of his entrance into the world.   By the time that the first and third Gospels were written, it is evident that the doctrine of the Virgin Birth had come to be widely held in the Church.   In the latter part of the second century a form of the text of the Johannine Prologue[6] was known in some quarters which reveals the perplexity that this silence had caused.   We have seen[7] what St. Augustine found as a unique religious discovery in the opening verses of this Gospel.   But we did not stop to consider the interesting form in which one of his quotations was made.   "Also I found there that God the Word, ' non ex carne, non ex sanguine, non ex voluntate viri, neque ex voluntate carnis, sed ex Deo natus est.' "   This textual variant, which clearly refers to the belief that our Lord

---

[1] 1 John v. 4.   [2] John i. 14.   [3] John iv. 6ff.
[4] John xi. 33, 35, 38.   [5] John xix. 28.   [6] John i. 13.
[7] See p. 57.

was born of a Virgin, had already been accepted
into some forms of the Latin version of St. John two
centuries before the time of St. Augustine. In the
latter part of the second century Tertullian [1] quotes
it and roundly accuses the Valentinians of tampering
with the true text in the interests of their Gnostic
heresy. Irenaeus,[2] also, cites the passage in this form
four times. The Old Latin text of the Codex Vero-
nensis (*b*), of the fifth century, and one of the best
representatives of the European type of the pre-Vulgate
text, has it. There are also two possible passages in
Justin Martyr,[3] with doubtful support from five others,[4]
which might be allusions to this form of the text.
Within the last twenty years a complete text in
Ethiopic of a work called *Epistula Apostolorum*,[5] which
is believed to have originated in Ephesus about the
year 180, has been edited, and this seems, like Justin's
phrases, to have an echo of this reading. Apart from
the doubtful support of Justin, whose language is often
reminiscent of a passage in the Gospels rather than an
exact quotation, we have no scrap of evidence in Greek
that supports an allusion to the Virgin Birth in John i.
11–14. In spite of the great weight of such names as
Harnack, Blass, Loisy, Resch, and Zahn, who give
their vote in favour of the singular pronoun and verb,[6]
there are sound reasons for accepting the usual text.
Long before the middle of the second century the Virgin
Birth must have been an accepted dogma of the Church.
It is inconceivable that so valuable a proof text should
have been so successfully tampered with as to disappear

---

[1] *De Carne Christi*, xix. 24.

[2] III. 16, 2 ; 19, 2 ; 21, 5 ; V. 1, 3.   [3] *Dial.* lxiii. 2 ; lxi. 1.

[4] *Apol.* I. xxii. 2 ; xxvii. 9. *Dial.* liv. 2 ; lxxvi. 1, 2.

[5] Ed. by Carl Schmidt in *Texte u. Untersuchungen* (1919). See M. R.
James, *The Apocryphal New Testament*, p. 486.   [6] *I.e.* " who was born."

entirely from all our Greek MSS. of the Gospel had it formed part of the original text. On the other hand, while the usual text is in perfect accord with the Johannine teaching of regeneration,[1] this teaching has not been announced in the Prologue, and a scribe might easily expect to find a reference to the Virgin Birth at the opening of the Gospel.

Possibly in this connection we should notice the reference to his brethren (John vii. 3–9) who " did not believe on him," and to the words of Philip to Nathanael (John i. 45) and of the Jews at Capernaum (John vi. 42). The reference to Jesus of Nazareth as the son of Joseph may mean nothing more than the general supposition that Jesus was Joseph's son. But, as the Evangelist has a way of correcting the errors and misunderstandings which he has just reported, these may be further indications that the doctrine of the Virgin Birth had not yet reached the Church in which this Gospel took its rise.

In any consideration of the titles which Jesus claimed for himself in the Johannine representation, special attention should be given to the remarkable group of " I am " sayings. These are: " I am the bread of life," " I am the light of the world," " I am the door of the sheep," " I am the good shepherd," " I am the resurrection and the life," " I am the true vine," " I am the way, and the truth, and the life." [2] A new turn has recently been given to the significance of this group of sayings as a result of an investigation carried out by Professor Karl Ludwig Schmidt into the sayings in the

---

[1] As in John iii. 3–8 ; 1 John ii. 29, iii. 9, iv. 7, v. 1, 4, 18.

[2] John vi. 35, viii. 12, x. 7, 11, xi. 25, xv. 1, xiv. 6. In xi. 25 three important authorities omit the words, " and the life " (see R. V. G. Tasker, *J.T.S.* xxxvi. p. 390). Bernard (*in loc.*) gives strong reasons for their retention.

Synoptic Gospels in which the emphatic pronoun ἐγώ
is used on the lips of Jesus.[1] The contention is that the
Synoptic Gospels contain a number of sayings in which
we must recognize that Jesus, with undeniable insistence,
bears witness to himself. This is shown to be part of
the same claim which Jesus makes when he uses the
term Son of Man, speaking of himself in the third
person. With the argument as Professor K. L. Schmidt
carries it forward to the nature of our Lord's messianic
consciousness and the interpretation of the terms
Messiah and Son of Man, we are not now concerned.
It is well, however, that we should bear in mind that
these " I am " sayings in the Fourth Gospel have in
some respects their equivalent claims in the Synoptic
record.[2]

But more important than any other aspect of the
Christology of St. John is the place occupied in the
sayings of Jesus by the thought of unique Sonship.
Four times in this Gospel [3] and once in the First
Epistle [4] we find the word μονογενής applied to Jesus.
Two of these instances occur in the Prologue, and two
in our Lord's conversation with Nicodemus. Nowhere
else in the New Testament is the word used of Jesus,
but the three occurrences in Luke [5] and the passage in
the Epistle to the Hebrews [6] warn us against reading
any metaphysical significance into the word. That
warning is strengthened by the evidence of the Con-
cordance to the Septuagint and of the new Liddell and

---

[1] It forms part of his argument in " Jesus, Messiah and Son of Man,"
one of four lectures recently delivered in Denmark and published in
French under the general title, *Le Problème du Christianisme primitif*
(Paris, 1938).

[2] For a detailed discussion of these ἐγώ εἰμι sayings, see Bernard,
I.C.C. St. John, i. pp. cxvi.ff.   [3] John i. 14, 18, iii. 16, 18.

[4] 1 John iv. 9.   [5] Luke vii. 12, viii. 42, ix. 38.   [6] Heb. xi. 17.

Scott, and by the papyrological examples given in the
Vocabulary of Moulton and Milligan. The word means
"only of its kind," "unique," as does the word ἀγαπητός
in the Marcan account of the Baptism according to the
proofs set forth by C. H. Turner.[1] But this unique
Sonship is always presented as an incomparable
qualification for giving a full revelation of the Father.
It would be easy to multiply examples of the claim that
Jesus makes in the Fourth Gospel to unbroken filial
unity with the Father. The knowledge which he
displays, the marvellous powers which he exercises, are
not inherent in Jesus but are given him by the Father.
The words which he utters are not his own, but the
Father who sent him has given him commandment
what to say. The relationship is always expressed in
personal terms. On the Father's side there is love and
confidence. "The Father loveth the Son, and hath
given all things into his hand." [2] On the Son's side
the story reveals love and obedient trust. "The cup
which my Father hath given me, shall I not drink it?" [3]
The discourse in the Upper Room with its culmination
in the great Prayer sets forth most fully this profound
unity of will and understanding between the Father and
the Son.

There is, however, one passage with an important
bearing upon this theme which, when carefully studied
in the light of rabbinic usage, helps us to understand
the place which this filial consciousness has in the un-
congenial atmosphere of controversy. In considering
our Lord's answer to the charge of sabbath-breaking,
we observed that he made use of the rabbinic interpretation of the Divine sabbath-keeping, and claimed

that he performed judicial works as Son of Man as did his Father, such works as dispensing life, against which there was no close season. This infuriated the Jews, who charged him now with blasphemy, " because he not only brake the Sabbath, but called God his own Father, making himself equal with God." [1] Now it has been shown by Odeberg, [2] Schlatter [3] and others, that the formula, ἴσον ποιεῖ ἑαυτὸν τῷ θεῷ, corresponds exactly to the rabbinic expression which suggested to anyone trained in that mode of speech " to make himself independent of God," in other words, to rebel against Divine government. To this Jesus replies, in the paraphrase which Odeberg gives of verses 19ff.: " The Son does *not* ' make himself equal with ' the Father, he does not presume upon an independent authority. On the contrary, all his authority is derived from his Father. He is not a rebellious son, a blasphemer of the Divine Father ; on the contrary, his peculiar opposition is justified by his being and acting in absolute unity of intention and thought with his Father. His continual activity is not independent of the Father's activity ; on the contrary, he does the Father's works, he executes what the Father shows him, and commands him to do." [4]

The Johannine teaching about the HOLY SPIRIT is

[1] John v. 18.

[2] *The Fourth Gospel* (Uppsala, 1929), p. 203.

[3] *Die Sprache u. Heimat des vierten Evangelisten*, pp. 66f., *Der Evangelist Johannes*, p. 147.

[4] This is an illustration of the assertion repeatedly made by Dr. Israel Abrahams, the famous Talmudic scholar, that this Gospel preserves authentic discourses, especially in relation to the circumstances under which they are reported to have been spoken, thus enshrining a genuine tradition of an aspect of Jesus' teaching which has not found a place in the Synoptics. See *Cambridge Biblical Essays*, p. 181 ; *Studies in Pharisaism and the Gospels*, i. p. 12.

one of the most distinctive features of the Gospel. While revealing conceptions that are also found elsewhere in the New Testament, it presents a problem which is so complex that only the briefest outline of the questions which are raised can be offered at this stage. The scholar who has done most to explore the difficulties is the late Hans Windisch, who wrote three essays for three *Festschriften* which appeared within a few years of one another. " Jesus and the Spirit according to the Synoptic Tradition " appeared in *Studies in Early Christianity* ; [1] " The Five Johannine Sayings about the Paraclete " is an essay in the *Festgabe* [2] for Adolf Jülicher's seventieth birthday ; which was followed by " Jesus and the Spirit in the Gospel of John," a contribution to *Amicitiae Corolla.* [3]

The main points that attract attention are these. Apparently three conceptions are found in the Fourth Gospel of our Lord's relation to the gift of the Spirit. (*a*) First comes the witness of the Baptist (i. 32–33) : " I have beheld the Spirit descending as a dove out of heaven ; and it abode upon him. And I knew him not : but he that sent me to baptize with water, he said unto me, Upon whomsoever thou shalt see the Spirit descending, and abiding upon him, the same is he that baptizeth with holy spirit." No reader can fail to think of the Marcan narrative where at his baptism Jesus saw the Spirit descending upon him as a dove and heard the *Bath Qol.* Immediately after this

---

[1] A volume presented to Professors F. C. Porter and B. W. Bacon on their retirement from their chairs at Yale University. (Ed. by S. J. Case, New York, 1928.)

[2] Tübingen, 1927.

[3] A collection of essays offered to Dr. Rendel Harris on his eightieth birthday. (London, 1933.)

we read: "And straightway the Spirit driveth him forth into the wilderness." According to the Marcan account of the Baptist's preaching, his successor was to baptize the people with "holy spirit," to which Matthew and Luke add "and fire." There is little in the Johannine account of the work of Jesus to suggest that such a spirit-baptism was bestowed during his earthly ministry. In John iii. 34 Jesus says (not John the Baptist [1]): "For he whom God hath sent speaketh the words of God: for he giveth not the spirit by measure." Jesus characterizes his words as "spirit" and "life" (vi. 63). Again, if we combine Nicodemus's words in iii. 2 with our Lord's words in iii. 5, we may find a possible indication that the ministry of Jesus is regarded as a baptism with holy spirit.[2] (b) In chapter xx. there is the account of the insufflation. "He breathed upon them and said to them, Receive ye (the) Holy Spirit." This passage must be treated when we are considering the Church, the Ministry, and the Sacraments. This is an action recorded of the Risen Christ, and is quite distinct from the ministry of Jesus during the incarnate life. (c) But in a passage which is obviously the Evangelist's gloss, or that of an editor, we read at vii. 39: "This he said about the Spirit, which those who believed on him were to receive; for the Spirit was not yet (given), because Jesus was not yet glorified." This immediately follows a saying of Jesus: "If any man thirst, let him come unto me; and let him drink who believes on me." According to the gloss, Jesus could not fulfil this promise of conferring divine gifts before his glorification. It is in agreement

---

[1] See W. F. H., *The Fourth Gospel*, p. 126.

[2] In the opinion of some scholars the reference is to our Lord's own baptism in the Jordan.

with this point of view that the most characteristic teaching in this Gospel about the gift of the Spirit will be found. This is, of course, the teaching about the Paraclete [1] in chapters xiv.–xvi.

Windisch's special service has been to show that there are five Paraclete sayings which form a unity. The rest of the farewell discourse is complete, self-contained, and consistent without them. They interrupt the sequence of thought and represent a different conception. Without them we have a promise of a return of Christ to take his own to their home with him and the Father. With this we notice also that according to xvii. 13–17, "the word" is the legacy left to the disciples : "thy word is truth," by this "word" they will be sanctified. One result of this separation of the Paraclete sayings from the farewell address is immediately apparent. This will be studied in the lecture on "Eschatology and Mysticism." We must now briefly consider the meaning of the word Paraclete and then examine the five Paraclete sayings.

The etymology of the word Παράκλητος needs no discussion. It stands for one who has been called to the side of another. It is used in 1 John ii. 1 in the sense of Advocate (the "friend *at* court," as someone has put it). It is used elsewhere in the New Testament only in these five sayings in the Gospel. Here it represents the Holy Spirit given in Christ's stead to believers as a helper to bring them to God (the "friend

---

[1] It is to be wished that the example of the Rhemish version had been followed in thus transliterating the Greek word. Dryden's resounding version of the *Veni Creator* gives good literary sanction to this usage :

> O Source of uncreated heat,
> The Father's promised Paraclete.

from court ").[1] It is of interest to observe that the word Paraclete has been taken over and transliterated into rabbinic use in the form *P^eraqlēṭ* or *P^eraqlēṭā*, but its more frequent synonym is the Greek word συνήγορος similarly transliterated *S^enēgōr* and adopted. The opposite to this is the transliterated word *Qaṭṭēgōr* (κατήγωρ), " the accuser." No passage is to be found in rabbinic literature in which the word *P^eraqlēṭ* is expressly used of the Holy Spirit, but he is once named *S^enēgōr*, or advocate, which is actually indistinguishable from *P^eraqlēṭ*. Billerbeck's [2] discussion of this word may be summed up by saying that two passages show that the conception of the Holy Spirit as Israel's Intercessor was not unknown within the Old Synagogue, even if we cannot prove the actual use of the designation *P^eraqlēṭ*. There is therefore a close parallel to Rom. viii. 26, where the Holy Spirit is described as an intercessor, though the word Paraclete itself is not used.

The five Paraclete sayings are : (*a*) xiv. 15–17, (*b*) xiv. 25–26, (*c*) xv. 26–27, (*d*) xvi. 5–11, (*e*) xvi. 12–15.

(*a*) xiv. 15–17. The first may have been inserted in its present position (before verses 21 and 19), because it begins with the keeping of Christ's commandments as the test of love, and ends with the blindness of the world as the reason why it cannot receive the Spirit of truth. There are two links which connect this saying closely with the First Epistle. The phrase " another Paraclete " recalls 1 John ii. 1 : " If any man sin, we have a Paraclete with the Father, Jesus Christ the righteous." Secondly, after em-

---

[1] For this use of Paraclete with reference to Christ (Epistle) and also to the Holy Spirit (Gospel), *cf.* Rom. viii. 27, where intercession is ascribed to the Holy Spirit, whereas in verse 34 Christ is the intercessor.

[2] *Op. cit.* ii. 560–62.

phasizing obedience as the test of love, Jesus is represented as declaring that the disciples know the Spirit
of truth, "because he abides with you and shall be in
you." This indicates that in some sense a spiritual and
inward presence is promised of the *alter ego* of Him
who said, "I am the Truth." In the Epistle the words
about the Paraclete are immediately followed by the
words: "And in this do we recognize that we know
him, if we keep his commandments."

(b) xiv. 25–26. The second saying sets forth the
continuity of the work of the Paraclete with the
ministry of Jesus. The Paraclete is the Holy Spirit
whom the Father will send in the name of Jesus. He
will teach the disciples all things and will recall to
their memory all the sayings of Jesus. A ministry of
revelation is promised, akin to and a sequel to that of
the Incarnate Son.[1]

(c) xv. 26–27. The third saying brings the Paraclete
into closest relationship with both the Father and the
Son ("whom I will send to you from the Father").
He is further defined as "the Spirit of truth who pro-
ceeds from the Father." His function is to witness
about Jesus, and this is spoken of in connection with
the kind of witness which is already being borne by
those who have been in the fellowship of Jesus from
the beginning of his ministry.

(d) xvi. 5–11. The fourth saying contains two
statements. The first pronounces the impossibility of
a concurrent ministry of the two Paracletes. This is
not easily reconcilable with the conception that Jesus

---

[1] W. Michaelis (*Reich Gottes u. Geist Gottes nach dem NT.*, p. 31)
emphasizes the importance of this idea in xiv. 16, "another Paraclete."
"The Spirit is regarded as continuing the action of the historical Jesus
as Paraclete."

while on earth baptized with the Spirit. In itself it represents the truth that so long as the dominant personality of their Master was at their side the disciples could not grow to their full stature. Faith and obedience cannot have their perfect work until the visible fellowship has become an invisible communion, and a new sense of responsibility has developed within them severally and in their corporate life. In the second statement the Paraclete becomes the συνήγορος, the vindicator of Christ, and his action also as κατήγωρ, counsel for the prosecution, convicts the world, and thus reverses its erroneous judgement upon Jesus.[1]

(e) xvi. 12–15. The fifth saying, as the third, identifies the Paraclete (ἐκεῖνος) with the Spirit of truth. It recognizes the necessarily incomplete form of the incarnate revelation, which is limited by the present stage in the disciples' spiritual growth. The course of revelation will advance in the same direction until the Spirit of truth has guided them to the goal. As Jesus has in all his words and works glorified his Father, that is, has revealed his inmost nature and character, so will the Spirit bring to light all the grace and truth which their imperfectly trained vision has prevented the disciples from discerning in Him from whom the Father has withheld no treasure in the unsearchable riches of his love.

These five sayings form a unity. They are Johannine in form, but are they expansions of actual sayings of Jesus himself? The paucity of references to the Holy Spirit in the Synoptic record of the teaching of Jesus has often been observed. The most important pre-

---

[1] Cf. v. 45, where Moses is the κατήγωρ, with xvi. 8, where the Spirit fulfils this rôle.

diction relates to the aid which the Holy Spirit will give to the harassed disciples when challenged to bear their witness before the authorities of this world. This passage seems to belong to an early stratum in the traditional *Logia*. It is found in Q (Matt. x. 19f.; Luke xii. 11f.) and is among the sayings accepted as dominical which are interwoven with the Little Apocalypse in Mark (Mark xiii. 11f.).[1] It is noteworthy that in both the Matthaean and the Lucan parallels to the Marcan Apocalypse these words are not included, as they have already been recorded in another context. Further, while Mark gives them in the form, " It is not you who speak but the Holy Spirit," and Luke in the form, " The Holy Spirit will teach you in that very hour what you ought to say," Matthew preserves a form, " It is not you who speak, but the Spirit of your Father who speaks in you." The Matthaean context (the ordination charge to the Twelve) seems too early for predictions of pains and penalties imposed by ecclesiastical, royal, and imperial courts of justice. This subject would come to the fore as our Lord's ministry drew to its close. We have thus reason to believe that Jesus in the last stage of the training of the Twelve did prepare them for a time when, no longer depending upon his physical presence, they would be enabled to witness about Jesus through the Holy Spirit, the Spirit of the Father. Instead of being flurried and flustered by their imposing ordeal, they would enjoy inward peace, their hearts would not be troubled nor fearful, and the Spirit of God would give them a " glad fearlessness of bearing." [2]   This is

---

[1] See R. H. Charles, *Eschatology*, ed. ², p. 379; Streeter, *Oxford Studies in the Synoptic Problem*, p. 180, *The Four Gospels*, pp. 491f.

[2] παρρησία, see pp. 171ff.

exactly what we find in the early chapters of Acts.
Peter was " full of the Holy Spirit " when he addressed
the high-priestly family and the Sanhedrin.[1] The
comment on this speech is : " Now when they beheld
the παρρησία of Peter and John . . . they took knowledge of them that they had been with Jesus." But
before this, at the very beginning of the narrative of the
Christian Church, a promise of the Lord is quoted,
pointing to an impending baptism with the Holy
Spirit.[2] The experience of the disciples in those weeks
and months which followed the Resurrection and
Pentecost, and the interpretation so readily given to it,[3]
seem to presuppose some preparation in the days just
before the arrest and crucifixion.[4]

If it is probable that these sayings about the Paraclete
go back in substance to words of the Lord spoken at
the close of his ministry, it is certain that they bear
marks of long reflection and of the experience of the
Church. For two generations the Christian Society
had been the Fellowship of the Spirit. The Parousia
still lay in the future, but the Church was secure in the
possession of the Paraclete, whose continuance of the
teaching of Jesus means " that the eschatological
message of the historical Jesus has been extended as a
result of Easter and Pentecost, which, on a backward
look, now enable the Jesus of history to be seen in a new
light." " The development does not run in a direct
line from the historical Jesus to the exalted Christ.
The life of the historical Jesus is continued on a higher
plane, whilst the possession of the Spirit by the Church

---

[1] Acts iv. 8, 13.   [2] Acts i. 5, cf. Luke xxiv. 49.   [3] Cf. Acts ii. 33.
[4] Cf. W. F. H., The Fourth Gospel, pp. 228f. See now W. F. Lofthouse,
" The Holy Spirit in the Acts and Fourth Gospel," Exp. T., lii. pp.
334ff.

remains on the plane of the historical, so that John is
warranted in writing of a first and of another Paraclete." [1] He does not write, as St. Paul does in one
passage,[2] identifying Christ and the Spirit.   Much as
the Johannine pneumatology owes in some ways to the
Pauline enrichment of the primitive Christian view of
the Spirit, it is both more consonant with the feelings
of the earliest disciples, and yet more highly developed.
The Spirit was the gift of the heavenly Christ, actually
dwelling in the company of believers on earth, and
replacing their departed Leader.   He was more than
the pledge and foretaste of the future Kingdom.
Though with St. John we are still in the pre-dogmatic
stage of the Trinitarian teaching, the sayings about the
Paraclete carry us a degree farther than any other
writing in the development of the New Testament
doctrine of the Godhead.

[1] W. Michaelis, *op. cit.* pp. 31, 32.   [2] 2 Cor. iii. 17.

CHAPTER IV

MAN, SIN, AND SALVATION

" FAILURE of Nerve " is the title which Professor
Gilbert Murray gave to one of the chapters in his book
Five Stages of Greek Religion. He contrasted the serene
humanism of the great writers of classical Athens, say
Sophocles and Aristotle, with the changed relation to
the world shown by writers of the Christian era.
Certainly he found the same quality in both non-
Christian and in Christian writers, in the Gnostics and
Mithras worshippers, in Julian and Plotinus, as in the
Gospels, the Apocalypse or the Christian Fathers.
The new attitude is seen in the " rise of asceticism, of
mysticism, in a sense, of pessimism ; a loss of self-
confidence, of hope in this life and of faith in normal
human effort." [1] It is undeniable that Christian
thought is far removed from philosophical humanism,
but whether it can justly be described as pessimism is
another question.

Wilhelm Bousset, in his survey of the *Religion of
Judaism in the late Hellenistic Age,* emphasizes the strain
of Jewish dualism which Zoroastrian influences brought
into the apocalyptic literature with a much stronger
note of pessimism. But, at the very time when dualism
was receding in Judaism, he finds in the Fourth Gospel
and in the theology of Gnosticism the first signs of the
union of Persian dualism (the opposition of good and

[1] *Op. cit.*, p. 155.

evil deities) with the entirely different Greek dualism
(antithesis of the material and immaterial world),
resulting in a thoroughly pessimistic condemnation of
this lower world.   This is attributed to the conviction
that the Devil is the κοσμοκράτωρ τοῦ αἰῶνος τούτου, and
that this world is given over to Satanic wickedness.[1]

This statement seems to go beyond the facts.   The
actual word just quoted, κοσμοκράτωρ, is not Johannine,
but is found in the plural in the famous description of
the Christian warfare in Ephesians vi. 10–18.   It first
occurs in the Orphic hymns, it is absent from the LXX
and from Philo, but was transliterated and adopted
into the rabbinic vocabulary, especially for the " angel
of death."   The Johannine equivalent is ὁ ἄρχων τοῦ
κόσμου τούτου, and there can be no doubt that St. Paul
and St. John alike inherited from Judaism a view of the
world which goes back to the period of the exile, when
first Babylonian and then Persian ideas provided the
Jews with both an angelology and a demonology.   The
Zoroastrian myth of the eternal antithesis between
Ahura Mazda and Angra Mainyu coloured the
thought of the apocalyptic writers and introduced a
dualism which has left its mark upon the language
of the New Testament.   With regard to St. Paul's
designation of Satan as " the god of this world "
(2 Cor. iv. 4), and his allusion to " the rulers of this
world " (1 Cor. ii. 8), Johannes Weiss [2] raises the
question how far St. Paul has taken seriously the view
involved in these words, and to what extent they are
an integral part of his world of thought.   He points
out that for Paul, as for optimistic Parsism, the final
victory of God and his sole rule were assured.   " As a

---

[1] *Die Religion des Judentums*, ed.[3] (1926), p. 515.
[2] *Das Urchristentum*, p. 472 (E.T. ii. p. 603).

Jew he may previously have considered with deep pessimism Satan's rule over this world, but this is overcome now that the decisive blow has been struck." His monotheism may have been imperilled theoretically, but not actually.

The same may be said about St. John. Anything like a cosmological dualism is ruled out by the Prologue : " All things were made through the Logos and apart from him nothing came into being." The Johannine dualism is practical, not metaphysical.[1] The Gnostic antithesis of spirit and matter is repudiated once for all in the decisive declaration : " The Logos became flesh." The Gospel and Epistle conspicuously set before us a series of opposites, light and darkness, truth and falsehood, spirit and flesh, life and death, righteousness and sin. The entire conflict is summed up in the antithesis between God and the world.

" The world " is a term which St. John uses about a hundred times. It stands for the whole creation, but generally for the world of men. It is never thought of in the Greek sense of the ordered beauty of nature. Fra Lippo Lippi [2] has caught the very spirit of Hellenism in the words :

> This world's no blot for us
> Nor blank : it means intensely, and means good :
> To find its meaning is my meat and drink.

To St. John, on the other hand, the world is the mass of mankind mobilized in defiance of the Divine purpose. Its characteristic is creatureliness, yet it

---

[1] Cf. J. Wellhausen, Das Evang. Johannis, p. 123. " The dualism between light and darkness is synonymous with the distinction of good and evil, and has nothing in common with the opposition between God and matter in Philo."

[2] Poetical Works of R. Browning, i. p. 522.

raises its head arrogantly against the Creator. The world was made through the Logos, yet the world knew him not. " For this cause the world knoweth us not, because it knew him not." [1] It is blinded by hatred to Christ and his followers. " If the world hateth you, ye know that it hated me before it hated you." [2] " Marvel not, brethren, if the world hateth you." [3] Yet to those who reject this witness Jesus can say: " The world cannot hate you : but me it hateth because I testify of it, that its works are evil." [4] Jesus recognizes a deep cleavage between himself and this hostile society. " Ye are of this world, I am not of this world." [5] The confidence of the Church lies in the knowledge that " we are of God, and the whole world lieth in the evil one." [6] Finally, the delusive fascination of this passing show stands in fatal rivalry to the enduring will of God. " Love not the world, neither the things that are in the world. If any man love the world, the love of the Father is not in him. For all that is in the world, the lust of the flesh, and the lust of the eyes, and the vainglory of life, is not of the Father but is of the world. And the world passeth away, and the lust thereof ; but he that doeth the will of God abideth for ever." [7]

No wonder this description has sometimes been classified as pessimism. [8] But to St. John the world

---

[1] 1 John iii. 1.   [2] John xv. 18.   [3] 1 John iii. 13.   [4] John vii. 7.
[5] John viii. 23.   [6] 1 John v. 19.   [7] 1 John ii. 15f.
[8] Cf. John Bailey, 1864–1931. Letters and Diaries, p. 180. " (Sir Henry Hadow) says he horrified a clerical conference by saying that the man who first classed together in a common condemnation the world the flesh and the devil was a medievalist doing the work of the devil. ' God so loved the world,' and ' no man hateth his own flesh.' Such things are not said of the devil ; and what is good as well as bad ought never to be confused with what is merely evil."

so regarded is the world of men alienated from God, blind to his presence, and hostile to his rule. He looks in one direction and sees Vanity Fair, with its cheap glitter and its empty pomps, its corruption and its disillusionment, and he foretells its swift decay. He looks in another direction, and he sees society organized in stark opposition to God, refusing to accept the freedom of the truth, resolutely bent upon the destruction of the Christian witness, and animated by hatred against Christ himself and all who make confession of his faith. As he surveys that field he is equally confident of the issue, " To this end was the Son of God manifested, that he might destroy the works of the devil." [1] St. John never leaves God out of account. The Gospel is the epic of the conflict between light and darkness, with its culminating intensity at the Cross. The Epistle carries on the tale as the struggle between the Church and the World. *Fides Victrix!*

A comparison between St. Paul and St. John reveals some interesting points both of similarity and of difference in their views of human nature and sin. St. Paul is interested in the natural history of sin. In two chapters of the Epistle to the Romans he sets forth the orthodox Jewish doctrine of sin. In chapter v. he goes back by way of illustration to the story :

> " Of Man's first disobedience and the fruit
>   Of that forbidden tree, whose mortal taste
>   Brought death into the world and all our woe." [2]

But this is almost incidental. His main purpose is to magnify the saving sphere of Christ's redemptive work. Employing the conception of racial solidarity

---

[1] 1 John iii. 8.   [2] *Paradise Lost*, i. 1ff.

he assumes, with every Jew, the disastrous results of Eden,[1] and argues *a fortiori* the immeasurable racial effect of Christ's life and death in obedience to the will of God.   But in chapter vii. he dramatizes, with all the passionate intensity of a redeemed soul, the struggles of a religious zealot with the " evil inclination," the *yēṣer hā-rā'* of rabbinic theology.[2]

It is one of our difficulties in understanding the inner meaning of the Johannine writings that they are completely wanting in the autobiographical note which gives to the Pauline Epistles their rich human interest. The " mythological " element, by which the Devil is brought so prominently into the discussion,[3] adds to

---

[1] The teaching of Rom. v. is that death, rather than sin, was passed on by Adam.   *Cf.* Ecclus. xxv. 24, and see Oesterley's discussion in *Camb. B.*, pp. lviii–lxviii, or in *Apoc. and Pseudep. of O.T.*, i. pp. 310ff. For the Jewish doctrine of the origin of sin, see G. F. Moore, *Judaism* i. pp. 474ff.

[2] This must not be identified either with " original sin " or with the Augustinian *concupiscentia*.   The *yēṣer hā-rā'* (placed in the left kidney !) was a necessary part of man's constitution, the biological impulse of life, and was only evil when it got out of control.   R. Samuel ben Nahman includes it in God's " very good," and says that without it a man would not build a house, nor marry, nor beget children, nor engage in trade.   See G. F. Moore, *Judaism*, i. p. 482, also F. C. Porter's elaborate study in Yale Bicentennial Publications, *Biblical and Semitic Studies*, pp. 95–156 (New York, 1901).   For a full list of rabbinic citations see Strack-Billerbeck, *op. cit.*, iv. pp. 466–83.

[3] For a brief history of the idea of Satan, see H. Wheeler Robinson, *Religious Ideas of the O.T.*, pp. 180f.   " The identification of Satan with the Serpent of Gen. iii. does not seem to be made before the apocryphal Book of Wisdom.   ' By the envy of the devil death entered into the world ' (ii. 24)."   On this passage see the comments of J. A. F. Gregg (*Camb. Bible*) and also of A. T. Goodrick (*Oxford Church Biblical Commentary*) *in loc.*   See also G. F. Moore, *Judaism*, i. p. 478.   For a fuller history of the doctrine, see article, " Satan," in Hastings, *D.B.* (O. C. Whitehouse) and *E.Bi.* (G. B. Gray).   For the textual and exegetical questions raised by John viii. 44, see Bernard, *I.C.C.* ii. 313ff., and Bultmann, *Krit.-Exeg. Komm. Das Joh.-Ev.*, pp. 240ff.

the difficulty, for it is not easy to determine how far this is figurative in its use, and to what extent it is fundamental to the outlook of the Evangelist. There are passages in which we can readily understand the pictorial use of a figure ultimately derived from an alien religion. Diabolism was abroad in the world in his day as in ours. But that is not an adequate explanation. We must look more closely at one or two passages in which this reference is found.

The late Professor F. C. Burkitt confessed that he found something repellent in the attitude assigned to Jesus by this Evangelist in his discussions with the "Jews." "It is quite impossible that the historical Jesus of the Synoptic Gospels could have argued and quibbled with opponents as he is represented to have done in the Fourth Gospel." [1] This, no doubt, is the impression left upon the minds of many readers. Without discussing how far the occidental mind is in a position to appreciate the lines of reasoning which were appropriate and congenial to disputants with a very different background of thought from ours, we may at least observe that the Evangelist, or the source upon which he draws, gave a representation which, to his Jewish mind, was in no way derogatory to the Master whom he adored.

The passage contained in John viii. 21ff. describes a typical scene in the temple courts when Jesus engaged in discussion with Jews who followed the customary methods of rabbinical reasoning. First, we read that Jesus declared the contrast between the two realms, the spiritual kingdom that is above and the world below, asserting his own heavenly origin, as the "One Sent" into the world to reveal the Father who is true,

[1] *The Gospel History and its Transmission*, pp. 227f.

so that his own message of judgement is a faithful expression of the character of the God who is eternal reality. We then find that his audience falls into three classes. There are those who *believed in him*; that is, became his disciples. Next there are those who *believed him*; that is, were favourably impressed without committing themselves as yet to a decision.[1] To these Jesus addresses an appeal that they should continue in his teaching, becoming his true disciples until they have learnt the truth which brings deliverance from the slavery of sin. At this point a third group takes up the argument. These are the persistent hecklers who dispute his claims : and Jesus meets them on their own ground. He had touched them on their most sensitive spot when he spoke of freedom. That was exactly what the covenant between God and Abraham, their ancestor, had guaranteed to them. In the Torah they possessed a token of their freedom from idolatry and sin. Confident in their pedigree, they retort that they have never been in bondage. To this Jesus replies that physical descent is not enough. The practice of sin is in itself evidence of bondage to sin. Their actions

---

[1] See Bernard, *I.C.C.* i. p. 193, ii. pp. 304f., for the distinction between the two constructions πιστεύειν τινι and πιστεύειν εἰς τινα in John vi. 29, 30, viii. 30, 31. So J. H. Moulton, *Gram. of NT Greek*, i. p. 67, says that the variation in viii. 31 from the previous construction " cannot be accidental." Torrey, *The Four Gospels*, observes the distinction in vi. 29, 30 (p. 196), but treats the constructions as identical in viii. 30, 31 (p. 202). He translates the construction with the simple dative in Mark xi. 31 (Matt. xxi. 26) : " did you not believe him ? " On this passage F. C. Burkitt remarks (letter 30.8.10) that the Old Syriac translates " believed not in him "; the Peshitta, " believed not him." " The Peshitta is literal ; the Old Syriac gives the Aramaic idiom." Moulton was inclined to accept the Marcan passage as translation Greek. This can hardly account for the marked variation in the Johannine passages cited above. See also pp. 155ff. below.

betray their paternity.[1] The Jews resent the aspersion cast upon their legitimate descent from Abraham. Unlike the Samaritans, their lineage is beyond dispute. But they detect a deeper meaning in the words of Jesus, and add, on second thoughts, that their spiritual Father is God. For their history for centuries past tells of a heroic struggle against idolatry to maintain the truth of the Divine unity.[2] Again Jesus argues that they cannot claim Divine parentage, for their deeds deny it. Their attitude to him in resisting the truth which he revealed to them from the Father, and in resolving to put him to death, was quite consistent with the character of their father, the Devil, who rebelled against God whose kingdom is truth, and who was a man-slayer ($\dot{\alpha}\nu\theta\rho\omega\pi o\kappa\tau\acute{o}\nu os$) from the beginning. He is essentially false, and his native tongue is falsehood. His envy and malice brought disobedience and death to the human race. His children cannot welcome the revelation which comes from the only true God, and they are bent on compassing the destruction of the Son whom the Father has sent to bring light and liberty to the world of men.

Now, however tortuous this discussion may seem to the modern reader of the Gospel, it is most closely related to certain conceptions which seem to have been held in rabbinic circles, and it helps us to understand the Johannine teaching about human nature and sin. We have seen that St. Paul, a Jewish thinker with a special experience of spiritual struggle and upheaval to

[1] Just as St. Paul argued that Abraham is reckoned as the father, not only of his lineal descendants according to the flesh, but of those who also walk in the steps of that faith which our father Abraham exercised before he received the sign of the covenant (Rom. iv. 11-12).

[2] Fornication was often the symbol for idolatry in the O.T. With John viii. 41 *cf.* Jer. iii. 8, 9, Ezek. xvi. 26, 29, xxiii. 37.

colour his language, made use of two views of sin that
are found in Jewish theology, the mythological and the
psychological. St. John does not show a direct interest
in the origin of sin, but in this discussion two points of
view are strangely blended.

First, let us note that " in the rabbinical literature
the paternal-filial relation between God and man is a
common theme." In illustration, G. F. Moore [1] quotes
R. Akiba's words : "Beloved (of God) are the Israelites,
in that they are called sons of God ; still more beloved
in that it is made known to them that they are called
sons of God." "R. Judah (ben Ila'i) thought that the
name ' sons ' was given them only when they behaved
themselves like sons ; [2] but R. Meir refuted him by
quoting passages in which they are called foolish sons,
untrustworthy sons, breed of evil-doers, vicious sons—
but sons notwithstanding. Instead of its being said to
them, Ye are not my people, they shall be called sons
of the Living God. [3] The relation is not annulled by
sin." [4] It is evident, then, that the possibility of forfeit-
ing the filial privilege through sin was a subject of keen
interest.

Next we find that in Jewish thought it was not the
" evil impulse " itself which was the basis of sinfulness,
but man's bondage to the *yēṣer hā-rā'*. [5] The truly
righteous are those who show a mastery over this evil

[1] *Judaism*, ii. p. 203.

[2] For this sonship, which is ethical, and not merely racial, *cf.* Ecclus.
iv. 10.

[3] Jer. iv. 22, Deut. xxxii. 20, Isa. i. 4, Hosea ii. 1 (E.V. i. 10).

[4] *Cf.* Wisd. xv. 2 : " For even if we sin we are thine, knowing thy
dominion. But we shall not sin, knowing that we have been accounted
thine." On the last clause J. A. F. Gregg comments : " The point of
view is ideal, but it is only an anticipation of 1 John iii. 6, v. 18."

[5] *Cf.* Ecclus. xv. 11–20 and Oesterley's comments.

impulse, such as Abraham and certain of the patriarchs.
" Abraham," says Odeberg,[1] " is in particular the
prototype of a master of the yēṣer and is by himself a
guarantee of freedom from sin and the yēṣer hā-rā'."
Hence the true sons of Abraham (i.e. those who are
his " sons " and not merely the " seed " of Abraham)
will not be in bondage to sin. Perhaps the contrast
between the slave and the son is an allusion to the
difference in status between Isaac and Ishmael, though
both were his " seed," leading on to the climax : " If
the Son shall make you free, ye shall be free indeed." [2]

A further point to be observed is that the " evil
inclination " was sometimes connected with Satan,
and even identified with him, or with the " angel of
death," whom we have already seen to be one with the
κοσμοκράτωρ, the " ruler of this world." Thus " he
was a man-slayer (ἀνθρωποκτόνος) from the beginning." [3]

We may carry the line of thought a little farther, for,
according to Jewish teaching, God grants freedom from
the yēṣer hā-rā', and the standing of sons of God to those
who study the Torah and obey it. Now Jesus on
another occasion said : "The ruler of this world cometh;
and he hath nothing in me." [4] This is indeed the true
Son of God. Well might he say : " If the Son shall
make you free, ye shall be free indeed." [5] Is it fanciful
to see yet one more link in the chain of reasoning ? We
saw in the second lecture that one of the ideas emerging
in the Prologue is that the Logos is the new Torah,
taking over and superseding the functions of the old
Torah. In him is the perfect revelation of the Father.
This gives, therefore, added significance to the words

---

[1] *The Fourth Gospel*, p. 300. [2] John viii. 36.
[3] John viii. 44. *Cf.* 1 John iii. 12, 15. [4] John xiv. 30.
[5] John viii. 36.

spoken to those who were already paying heed to his teaching and his claims, " If ye abide in my word, then are ye truly my disciples ; and ye shall know the truth and the truth shall make you free." [1]

The Johannine dualism shows itself in a group of passages which appear to teach that men fall into two classes,[2] those who have the capacity for faith, and those who have not. We are reminded of the Pauline dictum : " But all men have not faith." [3] Sometimes there is a suggestion that some men are born spiritually deaf or colour-blind. Sometimes we seem to hear an undertone of determinism. " He who is of God hears the words of God " ; [4] the unbelieving Jews do not catch the sound because they are not of God. " Ye believe not, because ye are not of my sheep. My sheep hear my voice, and I know them, and they follow me ; and I give unto them eternal life ; and they shall never perish, and no man shall snatch them out of my hand." [5] " No man can come to me, except the Father which sent me draw him." [6] " There are some of you that believe not. (For Jesus knew from the beginning who they were that believed not, and who it was that betrayed him.) And he said, For this cause have I said unto you, that no man can come unto me, except it be given unto him of the Father." [7]

On the other hand, there are other passages which modify the impression left upon the mind by these sayings when they are isolated from the rest of the Gospel. The Incarnate Logos is " the true light which lighteth every man." [8] When this light came into the

---

[1] John viii. 32.
[2] *Cf.* Ecclus. xxxiii. 7–15, with Oesterley's notes (*ut supra*).
[3] 2 Thess. iii. 2.   [4] John viii. 47.   [5] John x. 26ff.
[6] John vi. 44.   [7] John vi. 64f.   [8] John i. 9.

world, " men loved darkness rather than light because
their works were evil." [1]   " You refuse to come to me
that you may have life." [2]   " Him that cometh to me
I will in no wise cast out." [3]   " For this is the will of
my Father, that every one that beholdeth the Son and
believeth on him, should have eternal life." [4]   In these
sayings the predestinarian tendency [5] that we have
detected in others is counterbalanced. Perhaps the
most characteristic utterance put on the lips of Jesus
to emphasize the place of human responsibility and
volition is the declaration : " If any man willeth to do
his will, he shall know of the teaching, whether it be
of God or whether I speak from myself." [6]

Behind all these sayings there lies one of the dominant
thoughts of the Johannine writings. This is the conception of judgement. The revelation of Jesus the Son
of God confronts men with a crisis in which a decision
is demanded. The response to that demand reveals
the origin of the man, whether he is ἐκ τοῦ θεοῦ or ἐκ
τοῦ κόσμου, of God or of the world, from above or from
below. On this side of his teaching, John's language
seems to have been influenced by contemporary religious movements. The same kind of dualism is found
among the Gnostics. But in the Gnostic myth, as
Bultmann [7] says, such a reproach as, " You cannot
believe," is really a rational aetiology. [8] For in this
case faith is not a genuine decision, but a recollection

---

[1] John iii. 19.   [2] John v. 40.   [3] John vi. 37.   [4] John vi. 40.

[5] It is in a different sense that J. H. Bernard writes (*ap.* John ix. 3) :
" the doctrine of predestination is apparent at every point in the
Fourth Gospel, every incident being viewed *sub specie aeternitatis*, as
predetermined in the mind of God." See his treatment of the fore-
ordination of events in scripture, *I.C.C.* i. pp. cliii.ff.   [6] John vii. 17.

[7] *Krit.-Exeg. Komm.* Das Joh.-Ev. p. 240.

[8] That is a reasoned deduction from the philosophy of origins which
formed part of the Gnostic systems.

of one's mythical origin. The Gnostic is φύσει σωζόμενος, a man naturally marked for salvation ; and the unbeliever is lost by reason of his evil nature.

The Johannine theology meets the situation with the doctrine of the new birth, or the birth from above. This conception is not essentially new. In the Synoptic teaching of Jesus, entrance into the kingdom of God requires conversion, that is, becoming as little children.[1] Paul declares that if any man is in Christ he is a new creation.[2]   John avails himself of a vocabulary which was well understood in the world of Hellenism.[3] The doctrine is set forth boldly in the Prologue. " To as many as received " the Logos, " he gave the right to become children of God, even to those that believe on his name, who were begotten not of blood, nor of the will of the flesh, nor of the will of man, but of God."[4]   The same theme is expanded in the conversation with Nicodemus. " Except a man be begotten from above he cannot see the kingdom of God. . . . That which is begotten of the flesh is flesh, that which is begotten of the spirit is spirit. Marvel not that I said to thee (σοι), You must (ὑμᾶς δεῖ) be begotten from above."[5]

This doctrine appears also in two epistles which must probably be dated earlier than the Johannine writings. James i. 18 reads : " Of his own will he brought us forth by the word of truth, that we should be a kind of first-fruits of his creatures."[6]   Three

[1] Matt. xviii. 3.   [2] 2 Cor. v. 17.
[3] See Additional Note B, p. 197.   [4] John i. 12f.   [5] John iii. 3, 7.
[6] In spite of Hort's vigorous contention that St. James looks back to the creation (regarding it "as a Divine birth in virtue of a Divine seed, which was also a Word of truth, by means of which all other words of truth were to enter man " : *The Epistle of St. James*, pp. 31–35), we must agree with J. B. Mayor, Windisch, Ropes, Dibelius, Moffatt (commentaries *ad loc.*), and Büchsel (*Joh. u. d. hellen. Synkret.*, p. 65, *Th. Wörterb. z. NT*, i. p. 671), that regeneration is the meaning here.

allusions to it occur in 1 Peter. " Blessed be the God and Father of our Lord Jesus Christ, who according to his great mercy begat us again unto a living hope by the resurrection of Jesus Christ from the dead . . ." (i. 3.) " Seeing ye have purified your souls in your obedience to the truth unto unfeigned love of the brethren, love one another from the heart fervently ; having been begotten again, not of corruptible seed but of incorruptible, through the word of God which liveth and abideth. . . . And this is the word of good tidings which we preached unto you " (i. 22–23). " Putting away therefore all wickedness and all guile, and hypocrisies and envies and all evil speakings, as new-born babes long for the pure spiritual milk, that ye may grow thereby unto salvation " (ii. 1–2).

We shall see in a later lecture [1] how this doctrine came to be linked with the sacramental interpretation of baptism. We must now point out two important results. First, in the Johannine teaching, just as in the Pauline, the Fatherhood of God, in a religious as distinct from a creative sense, is not universal. But whereas St. Paul fell back upon Roman law and the widespread ritual of adoption to illustrate the indescribable honour of those who could now cry Abba, Father, St. John avoids the word " son " and prefers the term " child of God," for he thinks not so much of status as of a new family relationship. Secondly, the First Epistle sets forth the moral implication of this doctrine. " Whosoever is begotten of God doeth no sin, because his seed abideth in him : and he cannot sin, because he is begotten of God." [2] " We know that

[1] Lecture VI. See also Additional Note B, pp. 197f.
[2] 1 John iii. 9.

whosoever is begotten of God sinneth not ; but he that was begotten of God keepeth him, and the evil one toucheth him not."[1] On the former text A. E. Brooke[2] remarks that here, as elsewhere, " the writer speaks in the absolute language of the prophet rather than with the circumspection of the casuist." [3] Perhaps we might say that St. John is thinking of the instincts of the new creation. Sometimes this thought is expressed positively and inversely. " Every one that doeth righteousness is begotten of God." [4] " Every one that loveth is begotten of God." [5] " Whosoever believeth that Jesus is the Christ is begotten of God." [6] Righteousness, love, faith : the negation of these is sin. In the latter passage (v. 18) it seems better to accept the reading αὐτόν rather than ἑαυτόν, and to take the difficult phrase ὁ γεννηθεὶς ἐκ τοῦ θεοῦ as referring to Christ. In both passages the thought is that conduct is an expression of true character. Just as the Devil " speaks out of his own," [7] according to his essential nature, so by contrast does he whose new nature is from God prove himself true to his Father in the family life which is now his inheritance. *Noblesse oblige.* But there is a further ground for the high expectation. Twice over in the great prayer in the seventeenth chapter of the Gospel Jesus prayed that his disciples might be kept. " Holy Father, keep them in thy name which thou hast given me." " I pray not that thou shouldest take them out of the world, but that thou shouldest keep them from the evil one." [8] Now we read, " He that was begotten of God keepeth them, and the evil one

---

[1] 1 John v. 18. [2] *I.C.C.* The Johannine Epistles, p. 90.
[3] *Cf.* Wisd. xv. 2, and see above, p. 90, n.[4]. [4] 1 John ii. 29.
[5] *Ib.* iv. 7. [6] *Ib.* v. 1. [7] John viii. 44.
[8] John xvii. 11, 15.

toucheth them not." The Lord is mindful of his own.[1]

" The actual impartation of the actual life of God is the core of the Johannine soteriology. It is this that makes the Gospel a gospel, and Christ the mediator of a real salvation. ' This is the witness, that God gave us eternal life, and this life is in his Son.' " Thus Robert Law[2] sums up the meaning of salvation as it is set before us in the writings of St. John. It is evident that, just as St. Paul found the central message of Christianity in salvation, which he illustrated by figures taken from the law courts, or from the temple where slaves paid the ransom price for their manumission, so for St. John eternal life is the supreme gift of God brought to man by Christ Jesus.

In what way did he view the office and work of Christ in relation to the bestowal of this gift upon men ? The first impression that the reader of the Gospel receives is that, whereas St. Paul sees Christ's redemptive work in relation to the tragic experience of sin, St. John writes of Jesus rather as the revealer of truth, drawing men to God by the disclosure of the Divine character. Yet this is a one-sided picture. Even in the Gospel there are several significant statements

---

[1] For the essential difference between Gnostic and Christian teaching see von Hügel, *The Mystical Element in Religion*, ii. p. 238. " If in our Lord's teaching we find no trace of a Gnostic desire for purification from all things bodily as essentially soul-staining, we do find a profound insistence upon purity of heart, and upon the soul's real, active ' turning,' conversion (an interior change from an un- or anti-moral attitude to an ethical and spiritual dependence upon God) as a *sine qua non* condition for entrance into the Kingdom of Heaven. And the Johannine teachings reaffirm this great truth for us as a *metabasis*, or moving from Death over to Life." 1 John iii. 14 sums up the ethical significance of regeneration in this Epistle, and is a striking parallel to 1 Pet. i. 22–23. [2] *The Tests of Life*, p. 56.

D

which point to the conflict against the world's sin as exacting the supreme sacrifice of our Lord's life, whilst in the Epistle the problem of sin and its solution occupy a more prominent place.

It is commonly said that such passages in the Gospel as point in this direction are either accommodations by the author to the orthodox views held in the Church, or that they are editorial insertions to adapt the Gospel to satisfy the popular interest in the death of Christ. In the Epistle there are two pregnant statements which lie behind all that is written on this subject. " Sin is lawlessness." [1] " All unrighteousness is sin." [2] The mission of Jesus is set forth in general terms, as though instruction had already been given on this cardinal theme. " Ye know that he was manifested that he might take away sins." [3] This reminds us of the kerygmatic formula in 1 Corinthians xv. 3ff : " For I delivered unto you first of all that which I also received, how that Christ died for our sins according to the scriptures." When we look for some more specific explanation of the way in which this mission was fulfilled, there are four passages which seem to give some clue to the writer's attitude.

(a) 1 John i. 9 : " God is faithful and righteous to forgive us our sins, and to cleanse us from all unrighteousness."

(b) 1 John i. 7 : " The blood of Jesus his Son cleanseth us from all sin."

(c) 1 John iv. 10 : " God loved us and sent his own Son as a ἱλασμός for our sins."

(d) 1 John ii. 2 : " Jesus Christ the righteous is the ἱλασμός for our sins."

The fundamental idea in this Epistle is Fellowship

---

[1] 1 John iii. 4.   [2] Ib. v. 17.   [3] Ib. iii. 5.

in the Life Eternal. God is light, and there can be no fellowship with him on the part of those who walk in the darkness. It is a moral impossibility for sin and righteousness to dwell together in concord. The human desire for fellowship with God shown by the confession of sins finds that God, in accordance with his own character, faithful to himself " whose nature and property is ever to have mercy and to forgive," grants the forgiveness which delivers the soul from the anarchy of sin. The initiative, however, is throughout with God. It is he, in his boundless love, who has sent his Son to remove the barrier to this fellowship. For, as recent research [1] has shown, the word $\lambda\alpha\sigma\mu\acute{o}s$ (or its cognates) does not mean what the English word " propitiation " has come to mean. There is no thought of the placation of an angry Deity. This connotation may be found in the use of the word in classical Greek. But in the LXX it stands for the expiation of guilt, for the removal of that which makes approach to the holy God impossible. Moreover, righteousness is not only an attribute of God but an energy of God working for the salvation of men. Thus in the Deutero-Isaiah, God exclaims, " My righteousness is near ; my salvation is gone forth." [2] That active righteousness of God has become personal in his Son Jesus Christ, sent into the world as a $\lambda\alpha\sigma\mu\acute{o}s$ for our sins. It is He himself, not simply his death, that is the $\lambda\alpha\sigma\mu\acute{o}s$, so that the means of separation stands between God and man no longer. The cleansing thus thought of is not primarily the ethical change in character, though that is necessarily involved in the new relationship. Levitical ideas dwelt

---

[1] See C. H. Dodd, *J.T.S.* xxxii. (1931), pp. 342-60 ; *The Bible and the Greeks*, pp. 82-95.

[2] Isa. li. 5.

much on the thought of ceremonial, we might almost say technical, uncleanness, and expiatory sacrifices accompanied by the shedding of blood were largely concerned with such disqualifications. It was thus that the covenant relation was renewed. But according to Priestly theory, " the blood is the life," [1] and, as this ancient figure of speech is used by St. John, he thinks of the entire life of Jesus, showing forth the Divine glory, the character of God revealed in his will to save the world. But it is that life in the completeness of its surrender to the will of the Father.

When we turn back to the Gospel we find no such reference to the blood of Christ. The one passage which seems at first sight to imply this metaphor is the Baptist's exclamation : " Behold the Lamb of God, which taketh away the sin of the world." [2] This text is still the centre of seemingly endless controversy. Old Testament scholarship is invoked to remind us that in the Pentateuch there is no authority for the conception of a lamb as bearer of the people's sin. On the Day of Atonement their sin was borne away by the scapegoat. The one appropriate allusion seems to be the lamb led to the slaughter in the song of the Suffering Servant in Isaiah liii. This has indeed led to a most ingenious conjecture by two Aramaic authorities, C. J. Ball [3] and C. F. Burney.[4] They have pointed out the remarkable fact that the Hebrew word *ṭāleh*, " lamb," in its Aramaic form *ṭalyā*, means " child," " boy," " servant." The way has thus been opened for a suggested mistranslation. The Greek translator of this saying attributed to the Baptist mis-

---

[1] Deut. xii. 23, *cf.* Gen. ix. 4, Lev. xvii. 11.   [2] John i. 29.
[3] *Exp. T.* xxi. (1909), pp. 92f.
[4] *Aram. Orig. of F. G.*, pp. 104–8.

took the Aramaic word for its Hebrew cognate, and rendered it by ἀμνός instead of by παῖς, and thus the manifest allusion to the Suffering Servant of Jehovah was lost, to be replaced by the baffling reference to the Lamb of God. It has been suggested further that this change would be effected the more readily since the Servant whose life was made an offering for sin is also described in the LXX " as a sheep led to the slaughter, and as a lamb dumb before his shearers." The translator, however, who was sufficiently acquainted with the Hebrew word for " lamb," would probably know that ṭāleh does not occur at all in Isaiah liii, and that in the passage just quoted (Isa. liii. 7) the LXX rendering reverses the words for " sheep " and " lamb," and uses ἀμνός to translate rāḥēl, the Hebrew word for " ewe." It should be noted that Professor C. C. Torrey, whose keen scent for mistranslated Aramaisms in the Fourth Gospel had led him to detect no small number where most readers find the Greek text quite intelligible as it stands, has not included this example in his compendious list. Professor C. H. Dodd [1] favours the theory, disputed by Joachim Jeremias, [2] that the allusion is to the apocalyptic figure of the horned lamb, or young ram, which is found in Rev. xiv. 1, 2. But we have already seen [3] that both St. John and St. Paul seem to bear witness to an early Christian tradition that saw in the day and the hour of the death of Jesus a providential identification of Christ with the paschal lamb. This, of course, offers no solution to our problem, for the paschal lamb was not an expiatory sacrifice. Is it, however, necessary

---

[1] *Bulletin of John Rylands Library*, xxi. (April, 1937), p. 146.

[2] *Z.Nt.W.* xxxiv. (1935), pp. 115ff.

[3] See above, p. 21, and W. F. H., *op. cit.*, p. 154. *Cf.* 1 Cor. v. 7–8.

to postulate a clear, definite, and theologically precise use of that figure in the religious symbolism of Jewish Christianity ? The passover commemorated the great deliverance of Israel from the house of bondage. The Divine Figure which the new Israel commemorated in the Christian passover was the paschal lamb by God appointed, who said to them, as in symbolic fashion they took of the bread, " The bread which I will give is my flesh for the life of the world." [1] There is a complex of ideas, in which the original symbolism of the historic observance of Israel has been merged in a new Christian interpretation of the whole, and our Lord's identification of the Messiah with the Suffering Servant is the dominating factor.

Self-sacrifice, vicarious, but not expiatory, is a recurrent note in this Gospel. " For their sakes I consecrate myself " [2] is sacrificial language. " I lay down my life for the sheep." " The Father loves me because I lay down my life for the sheep that I may take it again." The voluntary nature of this sacrifice is emphasized. " No one has taken it from me. I have authority to lay it down, and I have authority to take it again. This command I received from my Father." [3]

When we attempt to see as a whole the Johannine conception of Salvation we are led inevitably to compare the total impression thus made upon our minds with that which follows from a reading of the Pauline epistles. The contrast in atmosphere and temperament is undeniable. St. Paul pours out a torrent of superlatives as he looks back in wondering gratitude at the

---

[1] John vi. 51.
[2] See Procksch, *Th. W. z. NT.*, i. p. 113 ; H. A. A. Kennedy, *Theol. of the Epistles*, p. 214.　　[3] John x. 15, 17, 18.

inconceivable mercy of God who, in the person of Jesus Christ, came to him and found him in the lowest depths of despair, only to turn the black and bitter shame of defeat into the most amazing victory. " O wretched man that I am? Who shall deliver me from the body of this death? Χάρις τῷ θεῷ διὰ Ἰησοῦ Χριστοῦ τοῦ Κυρίου ἡμῶν." [1] The very word for thanksgiving is the word for grace! And that is the keynote of the Pauline soteriology. These passionate outbursts of jubilation are not native to St. John. One might be tempted to apply the well-known classification of William James [2] (following F. W. Newman) and contrast these two writers as types of the " twice-born " and the " once-born " souls. But remembrance of the Johannine stress upon regeneration puts us on our guard against such a facile antithesis.

Grace is the word which sums up all that God's free and unmerited mercy has brought to St. Paul. Yet that word is never heard in the Fourth Gospel after the Prologue. There, however, in characteristically Johannine style, the theme of the Gospel is set forth in an arresting headline : " We have all been receiving grace after grace from his fulness." [3] As Dr. Moffatt [4] has happily put it : " This is another way of saying, ' By the grace of God I am what I am.' " To quote the same writer : " John does not connect ' grace ' with pardon or forgiveness as Paul did. But in the words ' Grace and truth came by Jesus Christ ' he is in line with the Apostle's idea that grace was the vital action of God and Jesus Christ, and that it referred not to creation, but to human nature in its deep need of the divine life." Again, when in the Gospel we meet

[1] Rom. vii. 24–25.   [2] Varieties of Religious Experience, p. 80.
[3] John i. 16.   [4] Grace in the N.T., pp. 367, 369.

so constantly the thought of 'receiving' we are brought back to the Pauline challenge : " What hast thou that thou didst not receive ? " [1]

It is otherwise with that other great Pauline statement in the vocabulary of salvation :   " God commendeth his own love toward us, in that while we were yet sinners Christ died for us," [2] or with that poignantly personal appeal, describing the transition from the old to the new life, in which the two foci of the elliptical orbit of his experience are so clearly marked :   " I have been crucified with Christ, yet I *live*, yet no longer I, but Christ *liveth* in me.   And the *life* which I now *live* in the flesh I *live* by *faith* in the Son of God who *loved* me and *gave* himself up for me." [3] How closely parallel are those Johannine sayings, " God so *loved* the world that he *gave* his only Son that whosoever *believeth* on him should not perish but have eternal *life*." [4]   " In this has the *love* of God been manifested in us that God sent forth his only Son into the world that we might *live* through him.   Herein is *love*, not that we loved God, but that he *loved* us, and sent his Son to be the means whereby our sins might be taken away." [5]

In both these pairs of sayings the love of God is thrown into the sharpest relief as the initiating and effective cause of life and of forgiveness.   The struggle over the perpetual validity of the old law has come to an end so far as the Fourth Evangelist is concerned. It belongs to the shadow land of

old, unhappy, far-off things,
And battles long ago.[6]

[1] 1 Cor. iv. 7.   [2] Rom. v. 8.   [3] Gal. ii. 20.
[4] John iii. 16.   [5] 1 John iv. 10.
[6] Wordsworth, *The Solitary Reaper*.

It is just because St. Paul's unyielding championship of the liberty of the Gentiles ended in complete victory that his forensic figures of speech are no longer current coin for St. John. We have passed from the law courts to the life of the home. Love, divinest love, is the foundation of the new fellowship, and grace following upon grace sustains us in the life eternal.

Chapter V

ESCHATOLOGY AND MYSTICISM

No aspect of the Johannine theology is more important
for a right understanding of the relation between the
Fourth Gospel and the rest of the New Testament than
the place which it gives to the doctrine of the last
things. Ever since Schweitzer's famous book forced
the eschatological question into the foreground of
Gospel studies it has been impossible to ignore the
subject. By "eschatology" is meant "that group of
ideas which is concerned with the catastrophe, or series
of catastrophes, which ushers in and accompanies the
end of the world."[1] The Jewish apocalypses were full
of such ideas, which they illustrated with a wealth of
symbolism that became part of the scenic properties of
all those who looked beyond the present evil age to the
final triumph of good over evil. With a thoroughness
that was logical rather than convincing, Schweitzer
attempted to interpret the entire life and message of
Jesus set before us in the Synoptic Gospels as controlled
by the thought of the immediate coming of the super-
natural Kingdom of God. In view of this impending
cataclysm all other thoughts fell into a subordinate
setting, and the ethical teaching of Jesus becomes only
a path leading up to the frontier of the Kingdom, after
which it is needed no more. This view, so startling to

[1] Sanday, *The Life of Christ in Recent Research*, p. 46.

those whose conception of our Lord's teaching about the Kingdom had been accommodated to the complacent assumption of a law of automatic progress, was by no means universally accepted. But it had this effect at least, that it compelled the student of the Gospels to recognize that there is much more in the teaching of Jesus about the Kingdom as a divine manifestation in the future than was generally allowed at that time.

It was still customary, however, to point to one of the Gospels as free from this Jewish conception of the reign and realm of God. The Gospel according to St. John was said to be the work of a mystic, who, from his own experience and that of a group of Christian disciples influenced by Hellenistic currents of thought, had shed all these obsolete expectations of the primitive Jewish Christian community, and lived in the calm enjoyment of direct communion with God through the risen Christ and his Spirit. It was assumed that eschatology and mysticism are antithetical and mutually exclusive.

So long as it was an almost unchallenged assumption that the roots of the Fourth Gospel were to be found in Hellenistic religion and not in Jewish Christianity, this was a simple method of interpretation. Nor can it be dismissed as altogether unreasonable. For the general impression left upon the mind of the reader is that no other book within the canon has fewer traces of the Jewish eschatological outlook. The reason for this superficial impression is to be found in the contrast which the Fourth Gospel presents on one side to the Synoptic Gospels with their eschatological colouring, and on the other to the Book of Revelation, steeped as that is in apocalyptic imagery. Probably there is a third reason ; for even the First Epistle of St. John, which obviously has the closest connection with the Fourth Gospel, bears striking evidence of the current Jewish and early Christian thought about the last things. Emphasis is thus given to the different outlook of the gospel. It is the unmistakable contrast in atmosphere and outlook between this Gospel and the Synoptics which has led to the exaggerated antithesis between mysticism and eschatology in the presentation of the teaching of Jesus.[1] In the Synoptics we have before us continually the figure of the Messiah and Son of Man, who is constantly speaking about the Kingdom of God. The apocalypse of Mark xiii. is preserved in Matthew, and, with whatever modifications, in Luke. There is nothing corresponding to this in John, but we have, by way of contrast, the Farewell Discourse where a mystical union is taught, and the coming of the Paraclete. It is not necessary to go to Schweitzer's extreme method of consistent eschatology as the one key to all the sayings of Christ to recognize the eschatological note as dominant in many a passage about the Kingdom, and to catch it as an undertone in many more. To give but one indication, the parables of the Kingdom are entirely unrepresented in the Fourth Gospel, and many of them draw their framework from the pictorial symbolism of the Jewish apocalypses. Such are some of the considerations which have led so many commentators to write about the elimination or transmutation of eschatology [2] in the teaching of Jesus as it is represented by the Fourth Evangelist.

[1] See Additional Note C, p. 201.

[2] " De-eschatologizing " would be an ugly parody of the German original, *Enteschatologisierung*.

Nevertheless, a closer examination of the Fourth Gospel brings to light a strongly eschatological element. Jesus as the Son of Man is commissioned with the functions of Judge and Giver of life. The spatial background of thought is the old Jewish apocalyptic contrast between the world above and the world below. The temporal framework of thought is partly concealed, but there are traces of the distinction between the two ages, the present age and the age to come. For it should not be overlooked that in such a passage as John xii. 25 (" he that loveth his life loseth it ; and he that hateth his life in this world shall keep it unto life eternal "), that favourite term in the Johannine vocabulary, " eternal life," is eschatological in its origin. In rabbinic language two technical terms are used antithetically, *hā 'ōlām hazzeh* and *hā 'ōlām habbā'*. These are equivalent to ὁ αἰὼν ὁ ἐνεστώς or ὁ κόσμος οὗτος, and to ὁ αἰὼν ὁ μέλλων. Now the term " eternal life," ζωὴ αἰώνιος, has the meaning, " life in the coming age," and it is understood so in the passage just quoted. In the same connection we should notice that chronological indications of τὸ ἔσχατον run through the Gospel. " The hour is not yet "; " the hour is coming and now is." Nor must we overlook the significance of the sublime cry from the cross, τετέλεσται.[1] Nothing, however, is more remarkable than the recurring refrain in the sixth chapter : " And I will raise him up at the last day."[2] The persistent attempts which have been made to cut these clauses out of the original Gospel is a pretty strong proof that the words do not fit unto the conventional view of the Evangelist's mind and spiritual inheritance. Again, is

[1] John xix. 30.   [2] John vi. 39, 40, 44, 54.

there not a kinship between the thrice-repeated promise in chapter xiv., " I come again," " I come unto you," " I come unto you," [1] and the long-cherished promise of the Parousia, " Yea, I come quickly," to which the expectant Church replied, " Even so, Lord Jesus, come quickly " ? [2]

In the third lecture it was pointed out that the five Paraclete sayings in chapters xiv.–xvi. form a unity, and that their detachment from their present position enables us to recognize more clearly that the subject of the farewell address is really the departure of Jesus and his return. It is the insertion of these Paraclete sayings in their present position which has obscured for the reader the main drift of that address by suggesting that the return of Jesus means nothing else than the gift of the Paraclete. The two ideas are complementary, not identical. There is nothing fundamentally inconsistent with the rest of the Gospel in the words that come near the end of chapter xxi. : " If I will that he tarry *till I come*, what is that to thee ? Follow thou me." Such, in briefest outline, is the statement for the eschatological colour of the Fourth Gospel. The case is strengthened when we examine some of the terms which are used again and again.

The term *Son of Man* occurs in eight different chapters, from the first to the thirteenth. The passages most significant for our purpose are : (*a*) John i. 51, " Ye shall see the heaven opened, and the angels of God ascending and descending upon [3] the Son of Man "; (*b*) John iii. 13–14, " And no man hath

---

[1] John xiv. 3, 18, 28.   [2] Rev. xxii. 20.

[3] C. C. Torrey (*The Four Gospels*, p. 318), on the basis of Job xxxiii. 23, renders the preposition underlying the Greek, " in the service of the Son of Man."

ascended into heaven but he that descended out of heaven, even the Son of Man. And as Moses lifted up the serpent in the wilderness, even so must the Son of Man be lifted up, that whosoever believeth may in him have eternal life " ; (c) John v. 26–27, " For as the Father hath life in himself, even so gave he to the Son to have life in himself : and he gave him authority to execute judgement, because he is Son of Man "[1] (d) John ix. 35, 39, " Jesus . . . said, Dost thou believe on the Son of Man ?[2] . . . For judgement came I into this world, that they which see not may see ; and that they which see may become blind " ; (e) John vi. 62, " What then if ye should behold the Son of Man ascending where he was before ? " ; (f) John xii. 23, " The hour is come that the Son of Man should be glorified " ; (g) John xiii. 31f., " When therefore [Judas] was gone out, Jesus saith, Now is the Son of Man glorified, and God is glorified in him ; and God shall glorify him in himself, and straightway shall he glorify him " (this is immediately followed by the words to the disciples, " Yet a little while I am with you. Whither I go ye cannot come ").

J. H. Bernard finds in the use of this term in the Fourth Gospel the same meaning which it bears in the Synoptics : " It was not a recognized term for Messiah, and was not interpreted as such ; rather was it always

---

[1] See R. H. Charles, *The Book of Enoch* (App. B. " The Son of Man," its origin and meaning) : " That the title, however transformed, had not parted with its apocalyptic meaning, is proved by John v. 22, 27, which are practically a quotation from Enoch lxix. 27." This verse is translated by Charles, *Apoc. and Pseudep of O.T.*, ii. p. 235 : " And he sat on the throne of his glory, And the sum of judgement was given to the Son of Man, And he caused the sinners to pass away and be destroyed from off the face of the earth, And those who have led the world astray."   [2] ἀνθρώπου is a better attested reading than Θεοῦ.

enigmatic to those who heard it applied by Jesus to himself. For him it connoted all that 'Messiah' meant, and more, for it did not narrow his mission to men of one race only. It represented him as the future Judge of men, and as their present Deliverer, whose Kingdom must be established through suffering, and whose gift of life was only to become available through his death." [1]

The term *Kingdom of God* in the Gospel is found only in the conversation with Nicodemus. But it is highly significant that in the two halves of the discourse of Jesus (separated by the misplaced [2] verses iii. 22–30) the first opens with the saying, " Except a man be born from above he cannot see the Kingdom of God," whilst the second half ends with the words : " He that believeth on the Son hath eternal life ; but he that obeyeth not the Son shall not see life, but the wrath of God abideth on him." Here we have the equation, " Kingdom of God " = " Eternal Life." So in the Synoptics " to inherit eternal life " and " to enter into the Kingdom of God " seem to be interchangeable terms. But whereas the Kingdom is the favourite expression in the Synoptics, Eternal Life, or simply Life, is the constantly recurring phrase in John. It is indeed true that the characteristic use of this term by St. John removes it from the region in which it took its rise. But the passage just quoted (John iii. 36) sets it in sharp antithesis to the wrath of God, ἡ ὀργή, which (as the Pauline epistles witness [3]) was a technical term in Jewish eschatology.

There is no more characteristic term in the Fourth

---

[1] *Op. cit.*, i. p. cxxxiii.

[2] See W. F. H., *The Fourth Gospel*, pp. 125ff.

[3] See Sanday and Headlam, *I.C.C.* Romans, p. 41.

Gospel than *Judgement*. The noun and the verb occur thirty-one times in the Gospel. Here again the prevalent use by the Evangelist may easily lead us to overlook such passages as John v. 21ff. This must be read in full, as it is the clearest evidence that can be adduced for the claim that there is a Johannine eschatology, and that it is an integral part of the Gospel. "For as the Father raiseth the dead and quickeneth them, even so the Son also quickeneth whom he will. For neither doth the Father judge any man, but he hath given all judgement unto the Son that all may honour the Son even as they honour the Father. He that honoureth not the Son honoureth not the Father which sent him. Verily, verily I say unto you, The hour cometh, and now is, when the dead shall hear the voice of the Son of God; and they that hear shall live. For as the Father hath life in himself even so gave he the Son to have life in himself; and he gave him authority because he is Son of Man.[1] Marvel not at this; for the hour cometh, in which all that are in the tombs shall hear his voice, and shall come forth; they that have done good, unto the resurrection of life; and they that have done ill, unto the resurrection of judgement."

While we shall be in small danger of overlooking the other conception of judgement which is regarded as almost peculiarly Johannine, we must not forget that there is a future as well as a present judgement in the thought of the Evangelist. This is best illustrated by John xii. 47ff., where the two conceptions are found side by side with no sense of incongruity. "And if any man hear my sayings and keep them not, I judge him not: for I came not to judge the world, but to save

[1] See p. 111, n.[2].

the world. He that rejecteth me, and receiveth not my sayings, hath one that judgeth him ; the word that I spake, the same shall judge him in the last day."

One other feature of the familiar Jewish and early Christian picture of the last things may be recognized in the words spoken in the farewell discourse. The *tribulations* of the last times by which the Messianic reign was to be preceded were the birth pangs of the new creation. So Jesus is represented in this last address as foretelling the woes through which the disciples must pass before the final triumph. " If the world hateth you, ye know that it hath hated me before it hated you. If ye were of the world, the world would love its own : but because ye are not of the world, but I chose you out of the world, therefore the world hateth you. Remember the word that I said unto you, A servant is not greater than his lord. If they persecuted me, they will also persecute you ; if they kept my word, they will keep yours also. But all these things will they do unto you for my name's sake, because they know not him that sent me." [1] " These things have I spoken unto you that ye should not be made to stumble. They shall put you out of the synagogues : yea, the hour cometh, that whosoever killeth you shall think that he offereth service unto God. And these things will they do, because they have not known the Father, nor me. But these things have I spoken unto you, that when their hour is come, ye may remember them, how that I told you. And these things I said not unto you from the beginning, because I was with you. But now I go unto him that sent me." [2] " A little while, and ye behold me not, and again a little while, and ye shall see me. Verily, verily, I say unto you, that ye shall

[1] John xv. 18ff.   [2] *Ib.* xvi. 1ff.

weep and lament, but the world shall rejoice : ye shall be sorrowful, but your sorrow shall be turned into joy. A woman when she is in travail hath sorrow, because her hour is come : but when she is delivered of the child, she remembereth no more the anguish, for the joy that a man is born into the world. And ye therefore now have sorrow : but I will see you again, and your heart shall rejoice, and your joy no one taketh away from you. And in that day ye shall ask me nothing." [1] " Behold, the hour cometh, yea is come, that ye shall be scattered, every man to his own. . . . These things have I spoken unto you that in me ye may have peace. In the world ye have tribulation, but be of good cheer : I have overcome the world." [2]

These quotations are given in some detail, because, familiar as they are to all of us, it is only when the more striking examples of the older eschatology are brought together in this way that we are in a position to feel their cumulative weight. This side of the presentation of the teaching of Jesus by no means dominates the Fourth Gospel. But it is there, and it is only by recognizing the part it plays in the general outlook of the Evangelist that we can go on to recognize the way in which many of the newer studies in both John and the Synoptics may lead us to that fuller grasp of the teaching of the early Church. It is a living unity for which we are feeling, in place of the older atomistic theology attributed to the writers of the several books of the New Testament.

First, there is only need to point out the bearing of this upon the recent attempts made in Germany by Rudolf Otto (in his book *The Kingdom of God and the Son of Man*), and in this country by Professor C. H.

---

[1] John xvi. 19ff.   [2] *Ib*. xvi. 32f.

Dodd (chiefly in his book *The Parables of the Kingdom*), to resolve the old antithesis between the teaching of Jesus as ethical and as eschatological by its interpretation as " realized eschatology."

To explain this term one cannot do better than show how Otto has emphasized the original element in Christ's proclamation of the Kingdom of God. He does this by drawing a contrast between Jesus and John the Baptist in their teaching and attitude towards it. Two points invite comparison. (*a*) Instead of a message of the menacing Day of Judgement Jesus brings the message of the Kingdom of God, which is good news. (*b*) Instead of the magical power of an eschatological sacrament with water Jesus proclaims the spiritual power of the ἔσχατον, the final order, of the Kingdom which has already broken in. And this was a characteristic of his teaching which later tradition obscured. In Otto's own words : " He is the eschatological Saviour. Only thus understood are all his deeds and words seen against their right background and in their true meaning. Directly or indirectly, they are all sustained by the idea of a divine power which breaks in *to save*. This idea has its immediate correlate in the new God whom he brings, the God who does not consume the sinner but *seeks* him ; the Father God, who has *drawn near* to men out of his transcendence, who asks for a childlike mind and a childlike trust, who frees not only from fear of the devil but from all fear and anxiety, who fills the entire life with childlike freedom from care." [1]

How far, then, did our Lord share in the current views about the Kingdom ? Otto's reply is : " The Kingdom of God is and remains for Christ the future

[1] *Reich Gottes und Menschensohn*, p. 83 (E.T., p. 107).

Kingdom of the final age, thought of in strictly eschatological terms, following on the 'Messianic woes,' following on the Divine Judgement. But what distinguishes his eschatology from that which had preceded it is, on the one side, that he already lives in the present active miracle of the final age, that with clear vision he sees this as something which is already coming into being and growing up around him, He knows himself to be supported by his powers already pressing on as an advance guard, and by their support and inspiration he works and preaches. On the other side, by his works, speech, parables, charismatic conferring of power, he mediates to a circle of disciples following in his steps, a contact with this miracle of the transcendent as a personal possession." [1] This is what is meant by the now familiar term "realized eschatology."

There is no need to elaborate the points of contact between this interpretation of our Lord's conception of the Kingdom as given in the Synoptic Gospels and the teaching of Judgement and Eternal Life set out in the Fourth Gospel. The powers of the age to come are already on the ground as an army of occupation. So the disciples of John the Baptist were to tell their master.[2] In the same way the " signs " in the Fourth Gospel tell their tale of the same powers in the hands of Jesus. The exultant cry that went up, according to St. Luke, when the Seventy returned with the report of their mission, " I beheld Satan fall as lightning from heaven," [3] is recalled by the Johannine " Now is the judgement of this world, now shall the prince of this world be cast out." [4] In each case the present victory

---

[1] *Op. cit.*, p. 123 (E.T., p. 155).   [2] Matt. xi. 4f., Luke vii. 22.
[3] Luke x. 18.   [4] John xii. 31.

sounds the death-knell of diabolic pretension. The decisive battle has been won, but the warfare is not yet accomplished.

Again, the parable of the Great Assize [1] might almost be an exposition of the saying in John xii. 47 : " If any man hear my sayings, and keep them not, I judge him not ; for I came not to judge the world, but to save the world. He that rejecteth me, and receiveth not my sayings, hath one that judgeth him ; the word that I spake, the same shall judge him at the last day." If we go on to ask what is that word which Jesus spoke, is not the answer to be found in the new commandment, "that ye love one another"? [2] For the explanation given to the wondering disciples, blessed of the Father, called to inherit the Kingdom prepared for them from the foundation of the world is this, " Inasmuch as ye did it unto one of my brethren, these least, ye did it unto me." Is this unrelated to the prayer : " Father, as to that which thou hast given me, I will that, where I am, they also may be with me ; that they may behold my glory which thou hast given me : for thou lovedst me before the foundation of the world "? [3] Mysticism and eschatology are united both in the parable which borrows its outline from the scene described in the sixty-second and sixty-third chapters of the Similitudes of Enoch, and in the prayer recorded in the Holy of Holies within the Fourth Gospel.

In the second place, it is well that we should recognize that, in varying ways, views at first sight inconsistent with one another are found side by side in other New Testament writings. The Epistle to the Hebrews, the most completely Hellenistic writing of all, sets forth, in

[1] Matt. xxv. 31-46.   [2] John xiii. 34, xv. 12, 17.   [3] John xvii. 24.

a way that suggests that the writer was trained in the school of Alexandrian Judaism, the Platonic conception of the two worlds, the world of reality in heaven, and the world of shadows on earth. But at the same time we find the Jewish time sequence of the age that now is, and the age that is to come. In this Epistle also the Christian believer already enjoys the powers of the age to come.[1] In the letters of St. Paul the dominant conception is that of the mystical union of the believer with Christ. Yet what could be more utterly Jewish than the short apocalypse in 2 Thessalonians,[2] or the eschatological sections in 1 Corinthians xv. ? Even in Philippians we meet with the watchword, " The Lord is at hand ! " [3] And in Romans [4] we meet with the significant saying, " Now is our salvation nearer than when we first believed."

In an essay on " Eschatology and Mysticism in Primitive Christianity," [5] Professor K. L. Schmidt remarks : " Paul is on the whole the cardinal point of the entire problem. In what way are eschatology and mysticism combined in him ? If we take his mysticism as the starting-point, then we have to speak of his experience of the immanent Christ, who will certainly be revealed completely only in the future. If, on the other hand, we start with his eschatology—and this method of treatment ought in any case to be carefully considered—then we have to speak of his hope in the transcendent Christ, who is already becoming immanent in the present. It is clear, whichever way our judgement goes, that the presence of eschatology and mysticism side by side in Paul and in primitive Christianity is certainly not a question of addition."

[1] Heb. viii. 2, 5, ix. 11, vi. 5.   [2] 2 Thess. ii. 1-12.   [3] Phil. iv. 5.
[4] Rom. xiii. 11, see below, p. 152, n.[3].   [5] *Z.Nt.W.* xxi. (1922), pp. 277ff.

There are two considerations to be touched upon, however briefly, without which the eschatology of the Fourth Gospel cannot be rightly understood in relation to the Synoptic and Pauline teaching on the one side, or to that of the First Epistle on the other.

(a) The eschatological appeal on the lips of Jesus in the earlier Gospels, as also in the Pauline letters, is a call to vigilance. " Watch, for you know not the day nor the hour." [1] So in the Fourth Gospel, where the present judgement dominates the thought, we meet with the same note of urgency, though the form of the appeal is not the same. Crisis overshadows the world. Men must walk in the light before darkness overtakes them. Obedient response to Jesus in faith must be given now. G. K. Chesterton's prayer,[2]

> From sleep and from damnation,
> Deliver us, good Lord !

sums up the challenge to watchfulness in the Synoptic and in the Johannine language.

(b) The change in emphasis between the eschatology of the Gospel and that of the Johannine Epistles may be summed up in two words. Judgement in the Gospel is κρίσις : in the Epistles it is φανέρωσις. But this φανέρωσις is implicit in the Gospel, and that is the true explanation of a certain strain in the teaching of the Gospel to which special attention has been called in this lecture.

The teaching of the Gospel is that in the historical Jesus the full glory of God was revealed to believers, and that by the response of obedient faith they received eternal life as a present experience. But it is also

---

[1] Matt. xxv. 13 ; cf. Mark xiii, 35, 37, 1 Thess. v. 6, 10.
[2] From the hymn, " O God of earth and altar."

shown that the glory of the incarnate Word was veiled from the eyes of the unbelieving ; that many disbelieved on him. So also the salvation, or eternal life, of the believers is hidden from sight. A final *dénouement* is impending to vindicate both Christ and those who are one with him. Moreover, Christ as a figure of history belongs to the past and to the present. He came forth from God, sent by him. He has gone back to the Father. The Johannine view of revelation demands that he should have a future if the historical revelation is to be fulfilled. That is why St. John has not given up his expectation of a consummation. This view is not emphasized as it is in the teaching of Jesus according to the Synoptic Gospels, or as it is by St. Paul. But, as Professor W. G. Kümmel of Zürich has well said : "If it is the essential nature of all primitive Christian eschatology to give expression to God's saving activity in Christ in the present and future, then for John the eschatology of the final scenes has a very important function. It does not speak of apocalyptic events or hopes, but it tells that the divine activity, which began in Christ's earthly life and his resurrection, will also at some time reach its glorious consummation, when all anguish, all distress, all death, will come to an end. And just because he holds fast to this expectation of the end, though it leads to contradictions, John takes his place in the organic unity of primitive Christianity. John is also, since the opposing motives must already have been so strong, a genuine witness for the primitive Christian belief in what God wrought on the plane of history for man's salvation in Jesus Christ." [1]

[1] "Die Eschatologie der Evangelien," *Theol. Blätter*, xv. (1936), p. 239.

To this we may add that, great as was the experience wrought through the Spirit in those who even now tasted eternal life, the looked-for φανέρωσις of Christ brought to John and to his readers an added incentive to the obedience of faith and love. " Beloved, *now* are we children of God. And it hath not yet been made manifest what we shall be, but we know that if he shall be manifested we shall be like him ; for we shall see him even as he is. And every one that hath this hope set on him purifieth himself, even as he is pure." [1]

If we are right in thus insisting that Johannine Christianity shares with the entire primitive Church in the eschatological hope, what room is left for mysticism ? Dr. W. R. Inge, in his Bampton Lectures on *Christian Mysticism*,[2] quoted a saying by Edouard Reuss to the effect that St. John cannot have used the phrase " the last day " in the ordinary sense, " because mystical theology has nothing to do with such a notion." While recognizing that those who believe space and time to be only forms of our thought must regard the traditional eschatology as symbolical, Dr. Inge contended that to credit St. John with the thought that, because judgment is now it cannot be in the future, is to foist upon him a view " which is destitute of any value, for it entirely fails to satisfy the religious consciousness. The feeling of the contrast between what ought to be and what is, is one of the deepest springs of faith in the unseen."

That is well said, and it opens the way for the more positive consideration. We have seen that one of the most important developments in recent New Testament study has been the recognition of " realized

[1] 1 John iii. 2, 3.   [2] (1899), p. 53.

eschatology " in the teaching of Jesus. If sometimes this interpretation has been carried too far, we have guarded against that by allowing for a future *dénouement* in the Johannine thought. But the early Church was faithful to the teaching of Jesus by expressing its belief that the powers of the coming age were already present in the manifest activities of the Spirit. St. Paul regarded the present possession of the Spirit as an "earnest" (ἀρραβών), that is, a pledge and foretaste in kind, of the future inheritance.

This is where the Paraclete passages find their true place in the Johannine message. They may have been inserted by the Evangelist in the farewell discourse in such a way as to interrupt the true sequence of thought. But their general context is right, for they form part of the eschatological hope. It is because of the sure and certain hope which is represented by the Parousia that a present union with Christ in the Spirit is possible. The work of the Spirit in teaching and inspiring the disciples to do even greater things than were achieved in Galilee is a continuation of the ministry of the incarnate Word. Between the departure of Jesus and his return the disciples of Jesus could experience what lay behind St. Paul's avowal : " I live, yet no longer I, but Christ liveth in me." [1] They could say : " We are in him that is true, even in his Son, Jesus Christ." [2]

At this point it seems necessary to state more clearly how this persistent eschatology is related to the philosophy that underlies the Johannine teaching. Professor Dodd is right in saying that " in the Fourth Gospel the crudely eschatological elements in the κήρυγμα are quite refined away. . . . The evangelist is

[1] Gal. ii. 20.   [2] 1 John v. 20.

deliberately subordinating the 'futurist' element in the eschatology of the early Church to the 'realized eschatology' which was from the first the distinctive and controlling factor in the κήρυγμα."[1] He is treading on more uncertain ground when he goes on to say: "The fact is that in this Gospel, even more fully than in Paul, eschatology is sublimated into a distinctive kind of mysticism. Its underlying philosophy, like that of the Epistle to the Hebrews, is of a Platonic cast, which is always congenial to the mystical outlook. The ultimate reality, instead of being, as in Jewish apocalyptic, figured as the last item in the historical series, is conceived as an eternal order of being, of which the phenomenal order in history is the shadow or symbol."[2] I gravely question whether, in spite of many points of contact with the Epistle to the Hebrews, the Fourth Evangelist fully[3] shares this Platonic view of the world. The underlying problem is that of the relation of time and eternity. This perennial problem of all philosophy haunts theology and demands attention more particularly when we are dealing with the Johannine type. The Hebrew approach (which is cardinal for the interpretation of St. John given throughout these lectures) seems to involve three positions : (a) the time-process is a reality, (b) closely related to "eternity," (c) which includes it rather than extends it, still less "shadows" it. Dr. Edwyn Bevan[4] points out that we must guard against an ambiguity when we speak of a future consummation. In some Christian-Jewish eschatological schemes the Messianic age on earth is conceived as the final phase of the time-process with a definite temporal duration.

[1] *Apostolic Preaching*, p. 155.   [2] *Ib*. p. 157.
[3] But see pp. 188f. below.   [4] *Symbolism and Belief*, p. 116.

But the consummation may be thought of as a state of being utterly unlike our present existence under conditions of material space, whether timeless or having unending duration. " The world process would get its meaning by leading up to it."   In meeting the objection of Bernard Bosanquet and Dr. W. R. Inge [1] that values are timeless and that the idea of a consummation is " to throw our ideals into the future," which " is the death of all sane idealism," Dr. Bevan illustrates his position from the Johannine theology. " It is perfectly true, of course, that a right relation to God in this world implies, according to the Christian view, the present possession of a great deal of ultimate good (the believer, St. John says, already has eternal life) ; but the Christian also insists that all present realization of good is imperfect, and that for the complete realization the Christian must look to the *future*. ' Beloved *now* are we the sons of God, and it doth *not yet* appear what we shall be.'   It is the combination of the ' now ' and the ' not yet ' which characterizes the Christian *Weltanschauung*." [2]

There is a further question to be answered. Is there not in the Johannine Epistles a special interpretation of the last things which is inconsistent with the teaching of the Gospel ? Five times in these Epistles the word Antichrist occurs, though it is found nowhere else in the New Testament. The idea itself is part of an ancient legend originating in Babylonian myth, reappearing in Jewish Apocalyptic, which has left its trace in 2 Thessalonians and the Book of Revelation. The passages which claim attention are : 1 John ii. 18— " Little children, it is the last hour : and as ye heard

---

[1] Recently urged in *God and the Astronomers* (see especially chapters iii. and vii.).   [2] *Op. cit.*, p. 117, n.

that antichrist cometh, even now have there arisen many antichrists ; whereby we know that it is the last hour. They went out from us, but they were not of us" . . .; (v. 22)—"Who is the liar but he that denieth that Jesus is the Christ ? This is the antichrist, even he that denieth the Father and the Son " ; 2 John 7— " For many deceivers are gone forth into the world, even they that confess not that Jesus cometh in the flesh. This is the deceiver and the antichrist." (*Cf.* 1 John iv. 2.)

The first thing to observe is how completely the writer has abandoned all the mythical and apocalyptic conceptions that clustered round the antichrist legend. He uses the word for the enemy who masquerades as the true interpreter of God, and deceives even the elect. But this is part of the primitive Christian tradition. Jesus is reported in Mark as saying : " Take heed that no man lead you astray. Many shall come in my name, saying, I am he : and shall lead many astray." [1] Luke adds these words : " The time is at hand : go ye not after them." [2]

Is not this the warning repeated by the Elder to the flock in their hour of peril ? Some seductive, deadly error is spreading within the Church. This must be the fulfilment of the ancient warning. And is there not in the Gospel a scarcely veiled warning of this very danger ? The saying in John v. 43 has been given some strange interpretations. " I am come in my Father's name, and ye receive me not ; if another shall come in his own name, him ye will receive." The ancient Church detected in this a prophecy of the antichrist. Modern writers have only too often found here a reference to false Messiahs and other political pretenders. One grotesque theory, which still persists, is that this

---

[1] Mark xiii. 6.   [2] Luke xxi. 8.

is a *vaticinium ex eventu* of the revolt under Bar-Cochba, that Messianic claimant who was recognized as such by R. Aqiba, the foremost rabbi of the age, and whose disastrous rebellion was put down by Hadrian in the years A.D. 132–35. Even that great historian of the ancient world, Eduard Meyer, lent his name to this theory in the first volume of his work on the *Origin and Beginnings of Christianity*, but in his third volume he wisely recanted.[1] It is interesting to see that Professor Bultmann, in his new commentary on the Gospel, says : " It is not necessary to assume that the Evangelist was thinking of any definite historical persons, in any case not of Bar-Cochba. For the ' Unknown Gospel,' whose fragments H. Idris Bell and T. C. Skeat have edited from papyri, and, above all, the fragment of John's Gospel edited in 1935 by C. H. Roberts, show that the Gospel according to John must have been known in Egypt somewhere about A.D. 100." [2]

With the abandonment of all such attempts to find in the Fourth Gospel contemporary references to messianic revolts in the second century we can the more readily see how closely the warning given in the Gospel accords with the Synoptic tradition. We can also recognize that the difference between the Gospel and the Epistles is the change from a vague prophecy to a clear recognition of its fulfilment in the supreme danger to which the Church is now exposed. At a time when others were looking out upon the political events of the age and were discerning in them a repetition of the events which called forth the first great Jewish apocalypse of Daniel, the Elder, true to the central thought of the Gospel, knew that the one

---

[1] *Ursprung u. Anfänge des Christentums*, i. p. 331 ; iii. p. 650.
[2] *Das Johannes-Evangelium*, p. 203, n.

supreme apostasy would be the denial of that truth which constitutes the Christian revelation and is the foundation of the Christian faith. He borrows the figure of the antichrist for this embodiment of craft and power, but beyond that he makes no use of apocalyptic imagery.

"The last hour." This is for him the ultimate crisis in history. And so he led the way in that long procession of visionaries who through the Christian centuries have sought scriptural support for this manner of stating the idea that the darkest hour precedes the dawn.

This was the text which Bernard of Clugny placed at the head of his famous rhythm, *Hora novissima, tempora pessima sunt, vigilemus !*

> The world is very evil ;
>   The times are waxing late :
> Be sober and keep vigil ;
>   The judge is at the gate :
> The judge that comes in mercy,
>   The judge that comes with might,
> To terminate the evil,
>   To diadem the right.
> When the just and gentle Monarch
>   Shall summon from the tomb,
> Let man, the guilty, tremble,
>   For Man, the God, shall doom.

CHAPTER VI

CHURCH, MINISTRY, AND SACRAMENTS

ABOUT the year A.D. 117 Ignatius, Bishop of Antioch, in the course of his journey to Rome to suffer martyrdom, wrote seven letters to churches in the provinces of Asia and Macedonia, and to Polycarp, Bishop of Smyrna. Anyone who turns to these letters to form some conception of Christianity as it was understood by one of the most prominent Christian leaders of the early second century will certainly be driven to the conviction that ecclesiastical order was the dominant interest. In every one of the six letters addressed to churches there are repeated references to the central importance of the bishop. Almost equally vital to the very being of the Church is the presbytery, whilst honourable mention is made of the diaconate. Even in the letter to Polycarp, where episcopal prestige might seem to need no emphasis, it is urged that nothing should be done without his approval,[1] and Polycarp is adjured that it is right for men and women who marry to be united with the consent of the bishop that the marriage be according to the Lord.[2] In the other letters we read that in church assemblies the bishop presides in the place of God, and the presbyters in the place of the Council of the Apostles.[3] Closely bound up with this constitutional doctrine is high sacramental

---

[1] Polyc. iv.   [2] *Ib.* v.   [3] Magn. vi., *cf.* Trall. ii., iii.

teaching. " Let no one do any of the things appertaining to the Church without the bishop. Let that be considered a valid sacrament which is celebrated by the bishop or by one whom he appoints. Wherever the bishop appears let the congregation be present ; just as wherever Jesus Christ is, there is the Catholic Church. It is not lawful either to baptize or to hold an agape without the bishop." [1] " Be careful to use one Eucharist (for there is one flesh of our Lord Jesus Christ, and one cup for union with his blood, one altar, as there is one bishop with the presbytery, and the deacons my fellow-servants)." [2] " Assemble yourselves together in common . . . in one faith and one Jesus Christ . . . to the end that ye may obey the bishop and the presbytery without distraction of mind ; breaking one bread, which is the medicine of immortality, the antidote that we should not die but live for ever in Jesus Christ." [3]

If we now travel back some twenty years to the middle of the last decade of the first Christian century, the Epistle of Clement, Bishop of Rome, to the Church at Corinth, shows a keen desire for the unity of the Church. It is not surprising that the descendants of those turbulent Corinthians, whose divisive tendencies gave such trouble to the Apostle Paul forty years before, needed a reminder once more of the parable of the body and its members. Again the duty of observing order in religious services is pressed upon them, and the writer goes back to the Old Testament institution of the central sacrifice at Jerusalem and the divine ordination of high priest, priests and Levites for the performance of sacrifices and services.[4] Then by a *tour de force* he discovers in this a divine warrant for the

---

[1] Smyrn, viii.   [2] Phil. iv.   [3] Eph. xx.   [4] 1 Clem. xl., xli.

institution of bishops and deacons.[1]   The apostles appointed bishops, making provision that if these should fall asleep other approved men should succeed to the ministry.[2]   Schism is doing great injury to the steadfast and ancient church of the Corinthians.[3]   " Only let the flock of Christ have peace with the presbyters set over it." [4]

About the time that Clement was writing to the church at Corinth the Gospel and Epistles of John probably saw the light.   Who can fail to be struck by the contrast !   The word " Church " is not used once in the Gospel, or in the First or Second Epistle, and in the Third Epistle only of the local church.[5]   The word " apostle " is used not once in the three Epistles, and only once in the Gospel in the general sense of " one who is sent." [6]   " Presbyter " is the title by which the writer of the Second and Third Epistles designates himself,[7] otherwise it does not occur.   The baptism of Jesus by John is not related in the Fourth Gospel,[8] but a confused sentence at the beginning of the fourth chapter says that Jesus was making and baptizing more disciples than John—" although Jesus himself baptized not but his disciples." [9]   The institution of the Eucharist is not recorded in the account of the last supper, nor is any eucharistic language employed in the five chapters devoted to the discourses in the upper room.   From the Epistles it might almost be said that ecclesiastical and sacramental language are wholly absent.

Nevertheless the Johannine writings contain teaching about the Church, the Ministry, and the Sacraments

---

[1] 1 Clem. xlii.   [2] *Ib*. xliii.   [3] *Ib*. xlvii.   [4] *Ib*. liv.
[5] 3 John 6.   [6] John xiii. 16.   [7] 2 John 1 ; 3 John 1.
[8] Though some discern a veiled reference to this baptism in iii. 5 (*cf.* 1 John v. 8—see below, p. 147).   [9] John iv. 1-2.

which is not the less important because it is indirect and
sometimes allusive. The evidence of the Pauline
epistles and of the Acts of the Apostles leaves no room
for doubt that all the writings of the New Testament
must be read against the background of the life of the
Christian Society. That was an ordered life, with
duly recognized ministries of service and administration, with a general outline of Christian teaching as
well as a traditional form of evangelic proclamation,
and with sacramental observances for the initiation of
converts and for the maintenance of fellowship with
one another by the common meal in which they shared
in the life of the Redeemer which he had poured out
in his sacrificial death.

(1) *The Church.* " The Bible knows nothing about
solitary religion." That remark made by " a serious
man " to John Wesley [1] might be abundantly illustrated
from the Johannine writings.

Professor F. C. Burkitt [2] found the history of the
embryo Church in the Marcan account of the breach
with the Synagogue and the Training of the Twelve.
We might trace the Johannine story of the beginning
of the Church in chapter vi., when many of the half-
hearted disciples " went back and walked no more
with " Jesus, who then said to the Twelve, " Would
you also go away ? " Simon Peter answered him :
" Lord, to whom shall we go ? Thou hast words of
eternal life. And we have believed and know that thou
art the Holy One of God." Jesus answered them :
" Did I not choose you the Twelve ? " [3] A company

[1] See the *Journal of John Wesley*, Standard Edition, i. p. 469 (n.).

[2] *The Gospel History and its Transmission*, pp. 76, 78.

[3] John vi. 66ff. It is significant that in Matt. xvi. 13-20 the announcement of the founding of the Church immediately follows Simon
Peter's confession of Jesus as the Christ.

of men, called and chosen by Christ, bound by a faith in his divine authority and receiving life from his words—this is the first stage in the Johannine conception of the Church. A further development is found in the allegory of the Good Shepherd, where the flock represents the Church—those who know the Shepherd's voice and follow where he leads, though they come from different folds, but in this way become one flock.[1]

In the fifteenth chapter the Church is represented by the allegory of the True Vine as the branches all deriving their life from the one stock, which is Christ. Unfruitful twigs are pruned away and fruitfulness is the test of vitality.[2] In this last discourse the unity of the Church and its separateness from the world are emphasized. But its unity is that not of an organization but of organic life. "Apart from me ye can do nothing."[3] No doubt that carries with it the thought that separation from the Church is fatal, but the stress is upon separation from Christ, whose vitalizing sap runs through every branch of the vine. The fullest expression of unity is found in the prayer of chapter xvii. In this chapter the description of the Church is, "those whom Thou hast given me," but on the first occurrence of this title the conception of a single corporate whole is placed in sharpest prominence by the phrase $\pi\hat{a}\nu$ $\hat{o}$ $\delta\acute{\epsilon}\delta\omega\kappa as$ $a\mathrm{\mathit{\dot{v}}}\tau\hat{\omega}$, "that entire unity which Thou hast given him," followed immediately by the plural, "that to them he might give eternal life."[4] What then can we learn about this corporate fellowship of disciples in the great prayer of this chapter?

(a) Christ has manifested the Father's name to those whom He gave to him out of the world, and has himself

---

[1] John x. 4, 16.   [2] Ib. xv. 1-2.   [3] Ib. xv. 5.   [4] Ib. xvii. 2.

been glorified in them.[1] (b) They have kept his word, they have received the sayings which Christ mediated to them from God, and they have faith in his divine mission.[2] (c) They are in the world with a mission to the world, but they are to be kept from the evil power which rules it, while sharing in the hatred which the world feels for Christ.[3] (d) Their mission is so to make known the word delivered to them that their hearers may believe, and thus be brought into the same unity.[4] (e) This unity is a fellowship of love which reveals and reflects the perfect unity of will and purpose that subsists between the Father and the Son.[5] (f) The witness of this earthly society of believers is to convince the world of the divine mission of Jesus Christ and the love of God shown both to his Son and to those who are thus united with him.[6] (g) For the consecration of the Church to this mission the Son is consecrating himself in the sacrifice of the cross, whilst the medium of this consecration is the Truth, the word of God, the fulness of the revelation of the Father in the Son. [7]

We saw in an earlier lecture[8] that in the five Paraclete sayings the work of the Spirit is set forth in his office as teacher and guide of the Church into its fuller apprehension of the truth revealed by the Incarnate *Logos*, and also as advocate in its task of witnessing to the world.

There is yet another figure used once in the Gospel, quite allusively, which we might easily overlook but for its use in other parts of the New Testament. The Church is the Bride of Christ. When the Baptist's disciples complained that more followers were now

---

[1] John xvii. 6, 10.   [2] *Ib*. xvii. 6, 8.   [3] *Ib*. xvii. 11, 14, 15.
[4] *Ib*. xvii. 20, 21.   [5] *Ib*. xvii. 22, 26.   [6] *Ib*. xvii. 23.
[7] *Ib*. xvii. 19.   [8] See pp. 75ff.

flocking to Jesus than to their own master, John replied : " A man can receive nothing unless it has been given him from heaven. He who has the bride is the bridegroom." [1] As Dr. Moffatt remarks : " The sequence of thought is at once intelligible when we recollect that in Oriental marriage the bride was commonly chosen for the bridegroom by the father. So the Church which gathers round Christ is the bride, appointed for him as a love-gift by the Father. The idea is the same as in vi. 37, where Jesus says, " All those will come to me who are the Father's gift to me, and never will I reject one of them.' " [2]

In passing from the Gospel to the Epistles we leave the conception of the Church as an ideal fellowship and face the actual conditions of Church life, with encouragements to rise to the privilege of " fellowship in the life eternal," and warnings against divisive tendencies and erroneous doctrines which would dissolve the faith. The Church is reminded of the hostility of the world and the peril of compromise with it. Disbelief in the reality of the Incarnation, failure to meet the demands of brotherly love, and the attempt to claim fellowship with the light while walking in darkness, are all inconsistent with the life of the Society that is in communion with Christ.

One other echo of the Gospel must not escape our notice. Fullness of joy is one of the notes of the true Church.[3] Herein lies the incentive to Christian witness. Those who have been entrusted with the word of life must share it with others. " What we have seen and

---

[1] John iii. 27, 29 ; cf. Mark ii. 20.   [2] Love in the N.T., p. 201.
[3] John xv. 11. It is reported of the philosopher Edmund Husserl that he put the question to a student thinking of giving up philosophy to become a pastor, " Can you preach joy ? " See Die Christliche Welt, June 11, 1932, p. 530. (I owe this quotation to Dr. Wheeler Robinson.)

heard we announce to you also, that you also may have
fellowship with the Father and with his Son Jesus
Christ. And these things we write to you that *our* joy
may be fufilled." [1] To preserve that fellowship as a
selfishly treasured monopoly is to lose the fullness of the
joy.

Two other notes of the Church are heard clearly in
the Fourth Gospel, even if they have sometimes been
interpreted in a way quite foreign to the Johannine
purpose. These are unity and universality.

It has been a misfortune in the history of doctrine
that in the allegory of the Good Shepherd, Jerome
translated the word ποίμνη, " flock," by *ovile*, " sheep-
fold." Thus, in the familiar language of the Authorized
Version, John x. 16 reads : "And other sheep I have,
which are not of this fold : them also I must bring, and
they shall hear my voice, and there shall be one fold
and one shepherd." " This fold " meant Judaism, and
the Evangelist certainly did not represent Jesus as
bringing Gentiles into the fold of the Jewish religion.
The universal scope of the Church is set forth in the
Evangelist's comment on the tragic irony whereby
Caiaphas's policy of expediency found utterance in a
reference to Christ's vicarious suffering. " Now this
he said not of himself : but being high priest that year,
he prophesied that Jesus should die for the nation ;
and not for the nation only, but that he might also
gather together into one the children of God that are
scattered abroad." [2] The universal extent of the
Church thus depends upon the universal purpose of

---

[1] 1 John i. 3, 4, ἡμῶν has far better MS. support than the v. l. ὑμῶν. It
also yields a finer interpretation. " In the spiritual harvest, sower and
reaper rejoice together." A. E. Brooke, *I.C.C.*, The Johannine
Epistles, p. 10.   [2] John xi. 52.

the self-offering of Christ, which is expressed again in xii. 32 : "And I, if I be lifted up from the earth, will draw all men to myself."

It is unfortunate also that the prayer for unity in the seventeenth chapter is so often quoted as though it referred to a uniform polity or to a centralized ecclesiastical bureaucracy. This thought also is quite foreign to the context. As Titius has said : "This unity is expected from the way in which believers are kept in the name of God, are in the Father and in the Son, are given the glory which belongs to Christ, and have the presence of Christ and therefore of God within them.[1] The perfect unity of the faithful is thus traced to the community of their life with Christ in all its relationships. It is thought of not in the manner of the Pietists as making for the isolation of each individual in his relationship to Christ, but as producing a community, binding individuals together into complete union." [2]

(2) *The Ministry.* The Johannine doctrine of the ministry, if we may so term it, is contained in four passages in the Gospel. (a) The double allegory of the Door and of the Shepherd in chapter x. (b) The acted parable of the foot-washing in chapter xiii. (c) The insufflation, with the word about the remission and the retention of sins in chapter xx. (d) The pastoral commission entrusted to Simon Peter in chapter xxi.

The first and the last place the emphasis upon the pastoral office. Taking the last first, we have the key to all the rest. To Peter the supreme charge is to act as a faithful shepherd. Whatever interpretation be

[1] John xvii. 11, 21-23.
[2] *Die neutestamentliche Lehre von der Seligkeit*, iii. 83.

E2

placed upon the famous words addressed to Simon after
his confession of the messiahship of Jesus recorded in
St. Matthew,[1] the significant point here is that in the
Fourth Gospel the Risen Christ gives a threefold
charge to Peter. Attempts have been made to dis-
criminate between the words used in the Greek for
" feed " and " tend " (βόσκω and ποιμαίνω), and
between " sheep " and " lambs " (προβάτια and ἀρνία).
In view of the Johannine mannerism of alternating
between synonyms,[2] there is as little need to distinguish
these pairs of words as to find an unnatural meaning in
the interchangeable words for " love " (ἀγαπάω and
φιλέω) in the same dialogue. The same charge is given
a threefold emphasis. Peter is to be a faithful pastor
of the flock.

The twofold allegory in the tenth chapter has been
strangely misunderstood. In the first part Jesus takes
up the words of the 118th Psalm, quoted messianically
elsewhere in the Gospels : [3]

> This is the gate of the Lord ;
> The righteous shall enter into it.

Combined with the Old Testament figure of Israel
as God's flock, the thought furnished Jesus with one
of the messianic " I am " sayings. As Westcott [4]
says : " The allegory is given at first in its complex form.
All the elements stand together undistinguished. Afterwards the two chief facts are considered separately, the
fold and the flock. In relation to the Fold, Christ is
the Door ; in relation to the Flock he is the Good

---

[1] Matt. xvi. 17ff.   [2] See W. F .H., *The Fourth Gospel*, pp. 120f, 254f.
[3] Ps. cxviii. 20.   Verses 22ff cited Mark xii. 10 (*cf.* Matt. xxi. 42f,
Luke xx. 17), Acts iv. 11.   Verses 25, 26 cited Mark xi. 9f. (*cf.* Matt.
xxi. 9, Luke xix. 38), John xii. 13.
[4] *The Gospel according to St. John* (1908), ii. p. 49.

Shepherd." Yet Dr. Moffatt, following the Sahidic version with no other support against the whole MS. authority, reads : " I am the Shepherd of the sheep " for " I am the Door of the sheep." To the same effect Professor C. C. Torrey [1] argues that confusion between similar Aramaic words led to the word " door " being given for " shepherd," with the further inference that verse 9, " I am the door : if any man enter by me, he shall be saved, and shall go in and out, and find pasture," is to be regarded as a later addition to the text, made necessary by the " error " in verse 7. All this seems gratuitous. Starting with the messianic claim to be the Gate, or the Door, Jesus divides the false from the true in those who claim to shepherd his people Israel. From the Old Israel he passes to the New. Who are those who may be regarded as the true shepherds of the flock ? Those who enter by the Door. His hearers were perplexed. Jesus explains : " I am the door : by me if any man enter in, he shall be saved, and shall go in and go out, and shall find pasture." This is the condition which determines the right of any man to the title of pastor. In Schlatter's words : [2] " The door is the main feature of the allegory, because at the door distinction is made between office usurped and office true, between false prophecy and the Word of God." The functions of the true pastor are then set forth in the description of the Good Shepherd. In contrast look at the figure of the hireling :

> Such as for their bellies' sake
> Creep and intrude and climb into the fold !

---

[1] *The Four Gospels*, pp. 207, 323f. See also his ingenious argument in *Our Translated Gospels*, pp. 108, 111ff.

[2] *Johannes der Evangelist*, p. 233.

> The hungry sheep look up, and are not fed,
> But swoln with wind and the rank mist they draw
> Rot inwardly, and foul contagion spread :
> Besides what the grim wolf with privy paw
> Daily devours apace, and nothing said.[1]

Over against this the shepherd who enters by the door is he who will lead forth the flock through the green pastures and beside the still waters.[2]

Next to this we have the acted parable of the foot-washing, in which again Peter is the conspicuous figure. This is the parable of humble service. Is it by accident that the Epistle which bears his name is not only that in which Christ is described as the Shepherd and Bishop of our souls, but that in which this pastoral aspect of the ministry is most fully set forth ? " Tend the flock of God which is among you, exercising the oversight, not of constraint, but willingly, according unto God ; nor yet for filthy lucre, but of a ready mind ; neither as lording it over the charge allotted to you, but making yourselves ensamples to the flock. And when the chief Shepherd shall be manifested, ye shall receive the crown of glory that fadeth not away." [3] These words might seem to be an exposition of the allegory of the Door and of the Shepherd. But the words which immediately follow are surely a reminiscence and an application of the " neglected sacrament " of the foot-washing. " Likewise, ye younger, be subject unto the elder. Yea, all of you, gird yourselves with humility, to serve one another." [4]

---

[1] Milton, *Lycidas*. Milton's allegory owes much to Spenser's *The Shepheard's Calender*, but far more to the Johannine original.

[2] The allusions in John x. 11ff. to Ezekiel xxxiv. are as numerous as they are obvious.

[3] 1 Pet. v. 2ff.   [4] *Ib.* v. 5.

πάντες δὲ ἀλλήλοις τὴν ταπεινοφροσύνην ἐγκομβώσασθε.
"Gird yourselves with humility as with the knotted
towel." [1]

There remains the difficult passage, John xx. 21-23.
"Jesus therefore said to them again, Peace be unto
you : as the Father hath sent me, even so send I you.
And when he had said this, he breathed upon them,
and saith unto them, Receive ye (the) Holy Spirit :
whose soever sins ye remit, they are remitted unto
them ; whose soever sins ye retain, they are retained."
The two points that concern us at present are : (a) To
whom were these words spoken ? (b) What is the
function entrusted to them in these last words ? In
answer to the first question we have Westcott's [2]
argument that there is nothing to limit the reference
to "the ten," whilst it appears from Luke xxiv. 33
that there was a general gathering of the believers in
Jerusalem. Hort, [3] while endorsing this, suggests that
even if the words were spoken directly and principally
to the ten, it was as representatives of the whole
ecclesia of the future that they received the Spirit and
were entrusted with the responsibility. [4] In regard to
the charge itself, we notice the Semitic form of the
expression, which closely resembles in meaning the
words in Matt. xvi. 19, and xviii. 18, where the rabbinic

[1] Even though the external evidence for the Petrine authorship is
not very early, the internal evidence seems to me all in favour of the
traditional authorship, which is maintained by Moffatt, *Introd. to Lit.
of N.T.*, pp. 331ff. See also F. B. Clogg, *An Introd. to the N.T.*, pp.
156ff. Those who are convinced by B. H. Streeter's ingenious conjectures regarding its date and composition (*The Primitive Church*, pp.
115-36) must allow for a common tradition drawn upon by the
Evangelist and the writer of one of the sources used by the editor of
1 Peter.   [2] *Op. cit.* ii. p. 350.   [3] *Christian Ecclesia*, pp. 32ff.

[4] For a full exposition of this passage see R. N. Flew, *Jesus and His
Church*, pp. 241-6.

terms " binding " and " loosing " are used.[1] It is
strange that here alone in St. John we find any mention
of forgiveness of sins. But the mission of Jesus was to
take away the sins of the world. Nevertheless Jesus
himself in this Gospel recognized sins of blind prejudice
and deliberate hostility to the light which shut men off
from eternal life.[2] There is therefore reason in Zahn's
comment [3] that the word of God in the mouth of the
disciples, as in the mouth of Jesus, is a two-edged sword.
But the saying surely goes further than that. It was
spoken in connection with the symbolic act of conferring the Spirit of Jesus upon his disciples. In the
life of that community part of the pastoral responsibility, of which much has already been said, is moral
instruction about the conduct that is required from
members of the Christian Society, and another part
deals with the exclusion of those who will not abide in
Christ and keep his new commandment, or who " sin
a sin which is unto death." [4]

The Third Epistle of John gives us a glimpse of the
ministry in some of its aspects. The Elder is obviously
one whose position entitles him to considerable influence in other churches than that of the city in which
he lives. Demetrius, in the words of G. G. Findlay,[5]
" is one of the ' messengers of the Churches '—travelling
apostles, prophets or evangelists—who passed from one
community to another and linked the Christian societies
together." As for Diotrephes, " who loves pre-
eminence " (ὁ φιλοπρωτεύων), H. J. Holtzmann [6] saw

---

[1] Probably a variant tradition of that logion. For the meaning, cf.
Streeter, op. cit., p. 36.
[2] John iii. 18, 35 ; viii. 21, 24 ; ix. 41 ; xii. 48.
[3] Kommentar zum NT. (1908), iv. p. 670.   [4] 1 John v. 16.
[5] Fellowship in the Life Eternal, p. 43.
[6] Lehrbuch der Nt. Theologie [2], ii. 434.

in him an unfortunate example of the monarchical episcopate. G. G. Findlay even conjectures : [1] " It is conceivable that Diotrephes was one of the first experiments in episcopacy, and that, puffed up by his new office, he had rebelled against his father in Christ and refused to take direction from Ephesus." In support of this theory it is mentioned that " the matters in which Diotrephes offends St. John—refusing to admit travelling brethren and attempting to ' hinder ' and even to ' excommunicate ' those who would entertain them—appear to have been originally a principal charge of the separated bishops, viz. the superintendence of hospitality and of inter-church relations." [2]

(3) *The Sacraments.* It is now generally recognized that it is impossible to read the discourses of the third and sixth chapters of the Gospel without finding in them a reference to the two sacraments of Baptism and the Eucharist. In view of the widespread sacramentalism of contemporary religious movements in the Graeco-Roman world the writer could not fail to know that such an interpretation must be put upon his language. It is just at this point that the closest resemblances to the Fourth Gospel are found in the writings of Ignatius and Justin Martyr.[3] If they have not borrowed Johannine language for sacramental purposes they have drawn on a common vocabulary in the Christian Church.

---

[1] *Op. cit.*, p. 42.

[2] B. H. Streeter, *The Primitive Church*, p. 85, says : " In this church Diotrephes held the office of Bishop in the full monarchical sense of the term." He regards ' the Elder ' as Bishop of Ephesus. "Indeed, to describe his office, the title ' Archbishop ' would—of course without the formal implications of later canonical law and usage—be even more appropriate than that of ' Bishop.' " *Ib.*, pp. 88f.

[3] See W. F. H., *The Fourth Gospel*, pp. 265f.

Two main reasons may be given for the reluctance of so many scholars of an earlier period to recognize the strongly sacramental tone of St. John. There are those who accept the discourses of Jesus as more or less authentic records, and feel that on his lips such references would be an anachronism. On the other hand, there are those who feel that the fundamental position of the Evangelist is that of a purely " spiritual " religion, in which faith brings the believer at once into a saving fellowship with Jesus Christ, so that any material medium is superfluous, if not contradictory, to the main teaching of the Gospel. At the present time the tendency of many scholars, who accept the view that the Johannine type of religion is mystical and immediate, is to acknowledge that there are sacramental allusions in the Gospel. They therefore use the critical knife to remove all such passages. Bultmann's new commentary is a conspicuous instance of this. He traces many passages to a later ecclesiastical redactor, who gained acceptance for the Gospel by bringing it into line with current usage and teaching in the Church. The worst of such a method is that it does not explain why the editor did his work so badly as to leave the strongest emphasis constantly on the teaching which is assumed to have been unacceptable. A far more probable explanation is to allow for both elements in the Gospel. We find the same problem in the letters of St. Paul. He assumes that admission into the Church is by baptism,[1] and tries to find a symbolism by which this can be related to the doctrine of the mystical union with Christ.[2]

[1] Rom. vi. 3ff.

[2] *Cf.* A. Schweitzer, *Paul and his Interpreters*, p. 213 : " The act and its effect are not bound together by religious logic, but laid one upon the other and nailed together."

But for St. Paul faith is always the determining fact by which the saving grace is appropriated. St. Paul also includes the story of the institution of the Eucharist as among the traditions which he handed on to the Corinthians.[1] In one chapter[2] he writes as though he accepted the current conceptions of the mystery religions about the physical results that may follow from sharing in a sacred meal. But in another chapter[3] he shatters any *ex opere operato* theory of sacramental grace by citing the fate of those Israelites who enjoyed baptism in the cloud and in the sea and were nourished with celestial food in the wilderness, and then perished miserably because of disobedience.

If St. Paul could write thus with no sense of inner contradiction, we need not wonder that both strains are found in one who wrote a generation later. By this time the Church (or part of it) had become so deeply sacramental that within half a generation Ignatius could write in the terms that have already been quoted. Yet the perils of such an attitude to sacramental grace were clear to this practical mystic. He was deeply responsive to the harmonious appeal of form and spirit. The symbolism of externals was but the fitting raiment of the interior meaning. Miracles were signs. Sacramental rites were more than merely pictorial representations.[4] There was an inner con-

---

[1] 1 Cor. xi. 23ff.   [2] *Ib.* xi. 30.   [3] *Ib.* x. 1ff.

[4] On the whole sacramental teaching of the N.T., including the Johannine, see the essay by C. H. Dodd, " The Life and Teaching of Jesus Christ," in *A Companion to the Bible* (ed. by T. W. Manson). Following up the argument by Dr. Wheeler Robinson on " Prophetic Symbolism " (*Old Testament Essays*, ed. by D. C. Simpson, pp. 1-17), Professor Dodd finds an analogous use of symbolical actions in the last week of our Lord's life on earth : the Triumphal Entry, the Cleansing of the Temple, and the Last Supper. Of the last, he writes : " In accordance with the nature of prophetic symbolism the significant act

nection. Baptism was the seal of faith. Only believers [1]
were baptized. He who believed in Christ received
eternal life. Life was the gift of the life-giving Spirit.
Therefore he that was begotten of water and the spirit
was in the kingdom of God. In like manner every
member of the Christian Church joined with his
fellows in the feast of communion, the outward sign of
the fellowship of the Spirit. There they broke the
bread and ate of the one loaf, thus symbolizing at the
same time the body of Christ given for them in his self-
offering for the world, and the unity of the Body of
Christ, that is, the whole company of the faithful united
in Christ their Head. But the actual death of Jesus
was the death of him who had come from above, the
Word become flesh.[2] They also drank the wine which
represented that life given for the life of the world.
Only those who entered by faith into the fellowship
of him who really became man and really suffered
death upon the cross could share in the spirit now
liberated from the body. " Verily, verily, I say unto
you, Except ye eat the flesh of the Son of Man and
drink his blood, ye have not life in yourselves. He
that eateth my flesh and drinketh my blood hath
eternal life . . . he abideth in me and I in him." [3]

No account of the Johannine teaching about the
Sacraments should ignore the stress laid upon the work
of the Spirit. In the third chapter the New Birth is

was not a mere illustration, but an ' efficacious sign '—in other words,
a sacrament " (*op. cit.* p. 386). *Cf.* with this R. Otto, *Reich Gottes und
Menschensohn*, pp. 253–8 (E.T., pp. 299–305).

[1] Or their families. *Cf.* Acts xvi. 31–4.

[2] For the rabbinical designation of the Torah as " bread," see
Strack-Billerbeck, *op. cit.* ii. p. 483.

[3] John vi. 53–6. See also Lecture VIII, p. 189, and Additional
Note D, p. 204.

mentioned four times. Twice it is referred to as birth from above. Once the form is, " Except a man be born of water and the Spirit." The last time the words are, most significantly, " So is every one that is born of the Spirit." That is where the final emphasis lies.[1] Similarly in the sixth chapter, the final emphasis is found in the sixty-third verse : " It is the Spirit that quickeneth ; the flesh profiteth nothing ; the words that I have spoken unto you are spirit, and are life."

There are those who think that the Epistle also contains an important sacramental allusion. Thus Hans Pribnow, in his brochure on *The Johannine View of Life*,[2] writes : " The Epistle also testifies to the inner connection between Baptism and the Spirit. As witnesses for the divine sonship of Jesus he names the Spirit, Baptism, and the Lord's Supper, but adds at once the explanation, $\kappa a\grave{\iota}$ $o\acute{\iota}$ $\tau\rho\epsilon\hat{\iota}\varsigma$ $\epsilon\acute{\iota}\varsigma$ $\tau\grave{o}$ $\overset{\text{"}}{\epsilon}\nu$ $\epsilon\acute{\iota}\sigma\iota\nu$."[3] This is the view taken by three of the best German expositions of the Epistle, those by Holtzmann,[4] Baumgarten,[5] and Windisch.[6] Yet Brooke objects that the three terms must be interpreted in verse 8 as in verses 6 and 7. He follows Westcott in recognizing the decisive reference in the aorist participle ($\acute{o}$ $\dot{\epsilon}\lambda\theta\acute{\omega}\nu$) to a past historic fact. Indeed, the two events which marked the opening and the close of our Lord's ministry on earth are inevitably called to mind, the baptism by John and the death upon the cross, when Jesus could say : " It is finished." " This is he that came by water and blood, even Jesus Christ ; not with the water only, but with the water and the blood."[7]

---

[1] John iii. 3, 7, 5, 8.   [2] *Die johanneische Anschauung von Leben*, p. 80.
[3] 1 John v. 8.   [4] *Hand-commentar zum NT*. (1893) iv. pp. 261ff.
[5] *Die Schriften des NT*. ed.[3] (1918) iv. p. 219.
[6] *Handbuch zum NT*. (1930) xv. pp. 132f.   [7] 1 John v. 6.

It is possible that the writer has in mind also the strange phenomenon recorded in the Gospel [1] because of its symbolical value, but that alone would not account for the statement that the " coming " of Jesus was effected by water and blood. Brooke [2] thinks that the tense of the participle " excludes any primary reference to the Christian sacraments." That is a cogent argument. Throughout both Gospel and Epistle the writer finds the secure foundation for the faith in the historical revelation of the Father made by his Son, when " the Word became flesh and dwelt among us." But the writer of the Epistle continues the thought. " And it is the Spirit that beareth witness, because the Spirit is the truth. For there are three who bear witness, the Spirit, and the water, and the blood : and the three agree in one." Westcott [3] points out that " the change of the preposition, the use of the article, and the stress laid on actual experience, show that St. John is speaking of a continuation of the first coming under some new but analogous form." He is surely no less true to the thought of the writer when he calls our notice to the change from the comprehensive description of the whole ministry of Christ in the previous phrase to the separate parts which have their peculiar witness in the experience of the living Church. We are thus led on to the ideas which underlie and are expressed by the two sacraments, that of " the water " and that of " the blood."

There is something in this allusive suggestion of the true place of the sacraments in the Church that is altogether in keeping with the Johannine method of instruction. In the third chapter of the Gospel the

[1] John xix. 34f.   [2] I.C.C., The Johannine Epistles, p. 135.
[3] The Epistles of St. John, p. 182.

context suggests that any baptism under discussion would be the baptism of John, which is contrasted with the true baptism with the Spirit. The teaching about the Lord's Supper is removed from the sacred context of its institution, perhaps because any controversial purpose would be strangely out of place in that hour of sacred fellowship. The discourse is set in a synagogue at Capernaum,[1] and in a conversation that followed. The main theme is the messianic gift of heavenly bread. The distinctive feature, brought in almost parenthetically, is the blood.[2] This interprets the previous dark allusion: "Yea and the bread which I will give is my flesh, for the life of the world."[3] It is the life laid down, the life of the Messiah who is also the Suffering Servant of the Lord. In the Upper Room the promise of the Spirit is given, the Paraclete who will take of the things of Jesus and make them known to his disciples.

At the end of the first Christian century the Church was passing through grave perils. There were those who too easily read into the Christian sacraments ideas which had their home in the altogether different climate of pagan mysteries. Others there were who denied the full historical manifestation of the Incarnate Word, or who disbelieved that Jesus underwent the actual experience of death as a true part of that divine revelation. Over against all these errors there stood the witness of the life of the Church and its sacramental testimony. The two sacraments were the two focal points in the Church's teaching. They also represented the initial step by which faith in Jesus, the same yesterday, to-day, and for ever, brought men into the

---

[1] John vi. 4 provides a significant context: ἦν δὲ ἐγγὺς τὸ πάσχα.
[2] John vi. 53. [3] John vi. 51.

living fellowship of the Christian Society, and the repeated act of communion by which the faith of the whole Church was sustained as it received again and again the sacred emblems of his passion. The life of the Church, taught, inspired, united by the Spirit, together with the acts that link the believer with the Lord whose earthly ministry began with the baptism and ended on the cross, form a threefold witness to the reality of the revelation made to the world in the Incarnate Word.

CHAPTER VII

FAITH, KNOWLEDGE, AND LOVE

THERE is no word in the rich religious vocabulary of the New Testament which expresses more aptly or more abundantly the common element that binds together all the diversities of early Christian thought and feeling than the term *faith*. According to the Synoptic Gospels the first demand that Jesus made upon men was that they should believe in the presence and power of the living God, and by simple trust in him banish care and fear from their lives, using without measure the powerful instrument of prayer which the Father places in the hands of his children. Where he found this eager temper of trustful confidence, Jesus rejoiced. Its absence stirred him to amazement, or plunged him into distress. In the presence of stolid unbelief even his will to heal was paralysed.[1] When we pass on from the earthly ministry of Jesus to the earliest days of the Apostolic Church we find that faith is so characteristic of the primitive community that the Christians are called " those that believed," or " the believers." The Western Text of Acts viii. 37 contains in the story of Philip's baptism of the Ethiopian what is perhaps the earliest form of the baptismal creed : " And Philip said to him, If thou believest with all thy heart it is possible ; and he answered and said, I believe that

[1] Mark vi. 5.

Jesus Christ is the Son of God." The word faith is
often used as a synonym for the Christian religion, as
we read : " and a great company of the priests were
obedient to the faith." [1] With Paul the noun and the
verb are both used to cover many aspects of the soul's
relation to God in Christ. Thus the initial step in the
Christian life is recalled when he writes : " Now is our
salvation nearer than when we (first) believed." [2]
Often faith is thought of as the response to the divine
grace which brings the believer into saving fellowship
with God, as in the statement : " For by grace have ye
been saved through faith ; and that not of yourselves ;
it is the gift of God." [3] This faith was so characteristic
of the Pauline churches that, whether writing to the
Thessalonians or to the Romans the Apostle could
rejoice that reports of their " faith " were spread far
and wide.[4] But in the light of his own experience of
the divine condescension in making known to him the
measureless love that stooped to death upon the cross,
faith for St. Paul had a far warmer personal meaning
than the acceptance of the historic fact of the redemption as true. Gratitude, devotion, complete self-
surrender, unwavering confidence in the Saviour, are all
united in this one word. Its fullest expression is found
in the words, " I live, yet no longer I, but Christ liveth
in me. And the life which I now live in the flesh I live
by faith in the Son of God who loved me and gave
himself up for me." [5]

In 1 Peter there are two passages in the first chapter
which set forth the special nuance of the word as it is

---

[1] Acts vi. 7.

[2] Rom. xiii. 11 (for the ingressive force of the aorist ἐπιστεύσαμεν,
see J. H. Moulton, *Grammar of N.T. Greek*, i. p. 109).

[3] Eph. ii. 8.   [4] 1 Thess. i. 8 ; Rom. i. 8.   [5] Gal. ii. 20.

used by this prophet of hope in a time when impending persecution threatened the Church. The future inheritance is reserved in heaven for those who enjoy the guardian care of God, and through the exercise of faith endure until the season of tribulation is past, and they can enter into that salvation which is now in readiness for them and will be revealed in God's own time. This hope brings joy even amidst the fiery trials, from the knowledge that what is genuine in their faith will be found more precious than the purest gold when the glorious revelation of Jesus Christ reveals also the real character of those who have been true to him.[1] Again, towards the end of the same chapter the writer speaks of Christ as revealed " at the end of the ages on your account, who through him are faithful, faithful I mean by resting on God who raised him from the dead and gave him glory, so that your faith and hope is on God." [2] We seem here to be nearer to the conception of faith which appears in the Synoptic Gospels. Thus in our Lord's words that follow the teaching about persistent prayer in the parable of the Unjust Judge the question is asked : " And shall not God vindicate his elect who cry to him day and night though he deferreth his anger on their behalf ? I say unto you, that he will vindicate them speedily. Howbeit, when the Son of Man cometh, shall he find faith on the earth ? " [3]

In the Epistle to the Hebrews again we find that faith comes near in meaning to hope, for it is stretching forward to grasp the prize that is promised to steadfast endurance. But it also represents confident trust

[1] 1 Pet. i. 3ff.   [2] 1 Pet. i. 20ff. (Hort).

[3] Luke xviii. 7, 8.   (See Field, *Notes on Translation of New Testament*, p. 72.)

in the unseen reality of God's present help. These two aspects of faith are brought out in the two noble definitions of faith given in the eleventh chapter : " Now faith is the title-deeds of things hoped for, the proof of things unseen." " For he endured as seeing him who is invisible." [1] For the Christian man, however, Jesus is " the author and perfecter of our faith." [2]

In the Pastoral Epistles faith is already passing over " into the sense of an acceptance of the truth of the Gospel, an assent to the testimony borne by the apostles to Christ, and even more generally the belief that God will do as he has said." [3] Nevertheless the authentic Pauline note rings out in such passages as 1 Tim. i. 16, 2 Tim. i. 12, iii. 15. In the Epistle of James faith is sometimes used as in the Synoptic Gospels, but also seems to mean little more than orthodoxy, whilst in the Epistle of Jude " the faith once for all delivered to the saints " is the deposit of apostolic teaching, a static conception far removed from the glowing enthusiasm of the Pauline faith. H. A. A. Kennedy called attention to the " very instructive fact " that in the Pastorals and James and Jude " the verb ' to believe ' (πιστεύειν), denoting the personal relation to Christ, and central in Paul, the Synoptics and the Johannine literature, is scarcely found at all." [4]

When we now turn to the Johannine writings, the first surprise that awaits us is the almost entire absence of the word for faith, πίστις. This noun is never used in the Gospel, or in the Second or Third Epistles. Once only do we meet with it in the First Epistle :

---

[1] Heb. xi. 1, 27. (See Moulton-Milligan, *Vocabulary*, pp. 202, 660.)
[2] Heb. xii. 2.   [3] H. A. A. Kennedy, *Theology of the Epistles*, p. 229.
[4] *Ib.*, p. 229, n.[1].

" This is the victory that has conquered the world, our faith." [1] Over against this must be set the striking fact that the word πιστεύειν, " to believe," " to exercise faith," occurs nearly one hundred times in the Gospel and nine times in the First Epistle. There must be some reason for this deliberate avoidance of a word which is found twenty-five times in the Synoptic Gospels, fifteen times in Acts, one hundred and six times in the Pauline Epistles, apart from thirty-three times in the Pastorals, thirty-two times in Hebrews, fifteen times in James, five times in 1 Peter, twice in 2 Peter, twice in Jude, and four times in Revelation. H. J. Holtzmann [2] thinks it an accident that the nouns πίστις and γνῶσις are both unused in the Gospel when the corresponding verbs occur so frequently. The reason for avoiding the noun γνῶσις when Gnosticism was already employing it as a watchword might seem to be self evident. It is not so easy to account for the absence of the noun πίστις. It is only used twice in the Corpus Hermeticum, so that we have no reason to suppose that it had acquired a meaning in contemporary Hellenistic mysticism which put the word under the ban. It seems more likely that the tendency in post-Pauline Christian use, to think of faith as a fixed deposit of truth, led St. John to prefer the verb. This stands for the active exercise of the higher judgement, with a certain moral force, in so far as it involves the taking up of a personal attitude to Christ. The verb πιστεύειν when used with a personal object was followed in classical Greek by the simple dative, whether the meaning was " to believe " or " to believe in." The evidence of the papyri shows that this was also the usage in the *Koine*. The usage in the Septuagint is rather different. The Hiphil *he'emīn*, " to make sure " or " to hold sure," [1] is the one Hebrew word for " to believe," and this could be followed by either of the prepositions *lᵉ* or *bᵉ*. In the Septuagint this Hebrew verb was rendered by πιστεύειν (or one of its compounds). If the preposition *lᵉ* was used in the Hebrew then the simple dative followed in the Greek, and, generally speaking, if the preposition was *bᵉ* then the Greek had ἐν with the dative. The idea of steadfastness or confidence lies in the Hebrew word, and *he'emīn*, translated again by πιστεύειν, is used absolutely in the sense of " to have confidence," or " to be hopeful." [2]

When we come to the New Testament we find a significant change. It is an impressive example of the way in which theology can sometimes determine grammar. When πιστεύειν is used for " to believe," " to give credence to," it is invariably followed by the dative alone. When it means " to trust," " to have confidence in," with the rarest exceptions it is followed by a preposition. Taking the New Testament as a whole, εἰς with the accusative is thus used forty-five times (of which thirty-seven are in the Gospel and First Epistle of St. John), ἐπί with the dative is used six times and with the accusative seven times (neither of which is represented in the Johannine writings). Of the thirty-nine times πιστεύειν is followed by the simple dative, eighteen instances are found in the Johannine writings. As J. H. Moulton writes,[3] " it

---

[1] From the verb *'āman*, " to carry," or " to sustain." For a careful examination of the lexical questions involved, see C. H. Dodd, *The Bible and the Greeks*, pp. 66ff.

[2] The Hebrew word most commonly used for " to have confidence " is *bāṭaḥ*, which in the LXX is rendered in this sense sixty-three times by πέποιθα and forty-seven times by ἐλπίζω.

[3] *Grammar of N.T. Greek*, i. p. 68. See also p. 88, above.

would seem as if the substitution of εἰς or ἐπί for the
simple dative may have obtained currency mainly in
Christian circles, where the importance of the difference
between mere belief and personal trust was keenly
realized." There are a few passages in both Gospel
and Epistle where the use of the simple dative comes
very near to the meaning elsewhere expressed by εἰς
with the accusative. But this is in keeping with the
special conception of faith in St. John, for confidence
and credence are more closely related here than elsewhere in the New Testament. Faith in the sense of
credence, that is, accepting someone's word without the
waverings of doubt, is given a high place where the
authority is self evident, or where spiritual insight
should discern the self-authentication of the message.
Thus : " He that heareth my word and believeth him
that sent me hath eternal life." " And ye have not
his word abiding in you : for whom he sent, him ye
believe not." " But because I say the truth, ye believe
me not." " And they believed the scripture, and the
word which Jesus had said." " For if ye believed
Moses, ye would believe me ; for he wrote of me.
But if ye believe not his writings, how shall ye believe
my words ? " " Beloved, believe not every spirit, but
prove the spirits, whether they are of God." Another
passage in the First Epistle shows the two uses in
contrast : " He that believeth on the Son of God hath
the witness in him : he that believeth not God hath
made him a liar." [1]

We have seen that in the Synoptic Gospels faith on
the lips of Jesus generally means complete confidence
in God. In the Fourth Gospel this thought is not

[1] John v. 24 ; v. 38 ; viii. 45 ; ii. 22 ; v. 46, 47 ; 1 John iv. 1 ;
v. 10.

so frequent, but John xiv. 1 is a link between the Synoptic conception and the more common Johannine claim for trust in Christ. Hort [1] renders this verse: "Believe, on God and on me believe," adding the comment, "the first suggestion being of constancy opposed to troubling and fearfulness (exactly as in Isa. vii. 9 ; xxviii. 16), and the second of the ground of that constancy, rest in God, itself depending on rest in Christ."

The object of faith in the Johannine, as in the Pauline, message is nearly always Jesus. This is one of the cardinal claims of the Fourth Gospel, for Jesus is represented as the Logos, the spoken word of God, who has been sent forth from God to reveal the divine character. Faith is the response of the human soul to the appeal and demand made by this revelation. To the question, "What must we do, that we may work the works of God?" Jesus answered, "This is the work of God, that ye believe on him whom he hath sent." [2] For in the first place this belief means moral discernment, freedom from prejudice and self-deception. In the Synoptic Gospels the sin against the Holy Spirit was that kind of stubborn resistance to the self-evident manifestation of goodness which was willing to put the most evil construction upon works of divine beneficence in the interests of a foregone conclusion. So the condemnation of complacent prejudice in this Gospel is heard in the words: "If ye were blind, ye would have no sin : but now ye say, We see : your sin remaineth." [3] It is this refusal to see, and the resulting perversion of the will, that constitutes the sin of unbelief. "He that believeth on the Son hath eternal life ; but he that disobeyeth the Son shall not see life,

[1] *Commentary on 1 Peter*, p. 83.   [2] John vi. 28f.   [3] *Ib.* ix. 41.

but the wrath of God abideth on him." [1] Hence it is
that the first work of the Spirit in the conviction of the
world is to force it to recognize that sin is not the failure
to comply with a code of moral regulations, but a false
attitude to goodness : " of sin, because they believe
not in me." [2] Yet this is far too abstract a thought to
do justice to the Johannine teaching. It is not merely
goodness that is in question, but the very nature of
God made visible in the Incarnate Word. Faith in
Jesus, faith in his name, involves certain affirmations
about him. It acknowledges him as Son of God and
Messiah,[3] as the Holy One of God,[4] as the Resurrection
and the Life.[5] It affirms his heavenly origin, his
divine mission, his essential relationship with the
Father.[6] This faith is the free response of man to the
revelation of God in Christ. It is a spiritual interpretation of what can only be spiritually discerned. Thus,
when Jesus says, "This too is my Father's will, that
everyone who beholds the Son and believes in him
should have eternal life," [7] he is not speaking of the
evidence of the bodily eyes so much as of the perception
of faith, which sees him for what he is.[8]

Yet there are several passages which seem to accept
a lower standard of faith by regarding miracles as a
foundation for belief. This appears to be in direct
conflict with the teaching of Jesus himself in the Synoptic Gospels. There faith was the condition required
for any mighty work to be wrought. In St. John
miracles are sometimes spoken of as though they were
intended to create faith. The dramatic representation

---

[1] John iii. 36.   [2] *Ib*. xvi. 9.   [3] *Ib*. xi. 27 ; xx. 31.
[4] *Ib*. vi. 69.   [5] *Ib*. xi. 25–6.
[6] *Ib*. viii. 23 ; xi. 42 ; xvi. 27, 30 ; xvii. 20, 21 ; xiv. 10.
[7] *Ib*. vi. 40.   [8] *Cf*. J. H. Bernard, *op. cit*. i. p. 201.

of our Lord's temptations in the wilderness, given in almost identical words in Matthew and Luke, sets down as Satanic a suggestion that Jesus should startle the populace into the acceptance of his messianic claims by a miraculous descent in the courts of the Temple and thus fulfil the expectation raised by Malachi's prophecy.[1] In complete harmony with this was his indignant refusal to play the rôle of miracle-monger. " This generation is an evil generation : it seeketh after a sign ; and no sign shall be given to it but the sign of Jonah. For even as Jonah became a sign unto the Ninevites, so shall the Son of Man be to this generation. The men of Nineveh shall stand up in the judgement with this generation, and shall condemn it : for they repented at the preaching of Jonah ; and behold, a greater than Jonah is here." [2] So also in the parable of Dives and Lazarus, the point is in the closing sentences. The first part of the story is borrowed from the folk-lore tales of Egypt and Palestine.[3] The distinctive feature is the request of Dives when he despairs of relief for himself. If a ghostly visitant from the other world were to appear to his brothers and warn them of their impending doom they would repent. " No," is the reply, " if they hear not Moses and the prophets, neither will they be persuaded, if one rise from the dead." [4] A belief into which a man is bludgeoned by some ocular demonstration which leaves him no course but to submit, has none of the moral quality of that faith which avails to the saving of the soul.

[1] Mal. iii. 1.   [2] Luke xi. 29–32.

[3] For H. Gressmann's important article on this parable, see J. M. Creed's commentary, *St. Luke*, pp. 208ff. Also Strack-Billerbeck, *op. cit.* ii. pp. 231f.; T. W. Manson, *Mission and Message of Jesus*, pp. 589f. ; B. T. D. Smith, *The Parables of the Synoptic Gospels*, pp. 64, 140f.

[4] Luke xvi. 31.

How different from this seems to be the Johannine Christ! " This beginning of signs did Jesus in Cana of Galilee, and manifested his glory ; and his disciples believed on him." [1] " Now when he was in Jerusalem at the passover, during the feast, many believed on his name, beholding his signs which he did." [2] " So the father knew that it was at that hour in which Jesus said unto him, Thy son liveth : and himself believed and his whole house." [3] What a contrast this version of the story offers to the account in Q, where Jesus commends the centurion before ever the miracle is wrought : " I have not found so great faith, no, not in Israel." [4] So also when the news of Lazarus's illness reached Jesus : " he abode at that time two days in the place where he was. . . . Then Jesus therefore said unto them plainly, Lazarus is dead. And I am glad for your sakes that I was not there, to the intent ye may believe." [5] At the close of that story comes the comment : " Many therefore of the Jews, which came to Mary and beheld that which he did, believed on him. But some of them went away to the Pharisees, and told them the things which Jesus had done." [6] Now when we look at these stories more closely, the meaning is not so clear as it seemed to be at a first glance. Those who were already his disciples were confirmed in their faith. But the opponents of Jesus were not converted by any of these marvels.

The same problem is raised by the claims which Jesus seems to make on the evidence of his mighty works. " If I do not the works of my Father, believe me not. But if I do them, though ye believe not me, believe the works : that ye may know and understand

---

[1] John ii. 11.   [2] John ii. 23.   [3] John iv. 53.
[4] Matt. viii. 10.   [5] John xi. 6, 14, 15.   [6] John xi. 45f.

F

that the Father is in me, and I in the Father." [1] But here the very next words show that Jesus was not attempting to force them into faith. "They sought again to take him." The real meaning of this appeal to his works is brought out by the words to the disciples in the farewell discourse. "Believest thou not that I am in the Father, and the Father in me? the words that I say unto you I speak not from myself: but the Father abiding in me doeth his works. Believe me that I am in the Father, and the Father in me: or else believe me for the very works' sake. Verily, verily, I say unto you, He that believeth on me, the works that I do shall he do also; and greater works than these shall he do; because I go unto the Father." [2] Jesus here appeals to his words and to his works as evidence of his unity with the Father, who works through him. If his assurance of fellowship with the Father does not convince them, they must consider his miraculous works. If those enable them to put faith in him, they will find the secret of effectual prayer and will possess the power to do the same things over a wider range than the limited field of their Master's earthly ministry. When Nathanael acclaimed Jesus as Messiah he was told: "Thou shalt see greater things than these. . . . Verily, verily, I say unto you, Ye shall see the heaven opened, and the angels of God ascending and descending upon the Son of Man." [3] On that passage Bultmann makes the comment that this is a mythological picture for the unbroken fellowship subsisting between Jesus and the Father. As no angelophanies follow in the Gospel, the view promised

---

[1] John x. 37–38. *Cf.* the Beelzebub controversy in Mark iii. 22–30 (Matt. xii. 24–32; Luke xi. 15–20).   [2] John xiv. 10–12.
[3] John i. 51.

to the disciples is not thought of as a vision of heavenly beings, but as the believing contemplation of his " glory," the vision of faith which sees the Father in him. This vision of his glory is promised in the entire ministry of Jesus, and in so far as particular miracles are part of this, they are to be regarded as evidence of the fellowship between Jesus and the Father.[1] We have already seen [2] that the Johannine conception of the δόξα of Jesus corresponds to the present possession by Jesus of the powers of the age to come. His eschatological messiahship is revealed by anticipation. The claim made by Jesus in John xiv. 10ff. is therefore a messianic claim which is in striking agreement with the answer to the delegation from John the Baptist as reported in Q : " Go tell John the things which you both see and hear." [3]   It looks, therefore, as though the Synoptic Jesus also allowed a place for his mighty works in the establishment of faith. When J. H. Bernard remarks about the passage under consideration (John xiv. 10ff.) that " the faith which is generated by an appeal like this is not the highest type of faith, but it is not despised by Jesus. Better to believe because of miracles than not to believe at all," we must observe, first, that this is not a peculiarly Johannine standpoint but is shared in the other Gospels ; and secondly, that it is not a quantitative so much as a qualitative test to which Jesus appeals. In him the powers of the messianic age are already at work, and they reveal his character as the One whom God has sent, and who is in perfect unison with the Father's will. It should be added that the Johannine Christ also deprecates the dependence of faith

---

[1] Bultmann : *Op. cit.* p. 75.   [2] See p. 117.
[3] Matt. xi. 4 ; Luke vii. 22.

upon signs. The exclamation, "Except ye see signs
and wonders ye will in no wise believe ! "[1] has quite
a Synoptic ring. Moreover, the last beatitude in this
Gospel is this : " Because thou hast seen me hast thou
believed ? Blessed are they that have not seen and yet
have believed."[2]

What then is the place of *Knowledge* in the Christian
experience, and how does it stand related to Faith ?
The well-known lines,

> We have but faith, we cannot know,
> For knowledge is of things we see,[3]

would be unintelligible in the Johannine circle. In
the New Testament generally, as also in St. John,
faith and sight are certainly opposed to one another.[4]
But faith and knowledge are far more closely related.[5]
Thus Peter's confession says, " We have believed and
know that thou art the Holy One of God," [6] whereas
we read in the First Epistle,[7] " We know and have
believed the love which God hath in us." Commenting
on the former, Bernard [8] says : " While John does not
lay down formulae as to the relative precedence of
faith and *knowledge* in regard to the things of the
spirit, his teaching is nearer the *credo ut intelligam* of the
saints than the *intelligo ut credam* of the philosophers.

---

[1] John iv. 48.   [2] John xx. 29.   [3] Tennyson, *In Memoriam* (Prologue).
[4] *Cf.* John xx. 29, just cited, with 2 Cor. v. 7. But St. John also uses
the verb " to see " of a mystic discernment. In like manner, " to
know " is not used in the strongly intellectual sense. For the relation
between θεωρεῖν, γινώσκειν and πιστεύειν in St. John, see Bousset, *Kyrios
Christos*,[2] pp. 171f.
[5] "The entire N.T. knows nothing of the modern ' either—or '
antithesis of faith and knowledge." H. J. Holtzmann, *Lehrb. d. Nt.
Theologie*, ii. p. 536, n. 1.   [6] John vi. 9.   [7] 1 John iv. 16.
[8] *I.C.C.*, St. John, i. p. 222.

The apostles had 'believed' in Jesus, and therefore they 'knew' who He was." On the latter text A. E. Brooke [1] supposes an allusion to those "early experiences in Galilee or Jerusalem, when growing acquaintance passed into assured faith, which had never since been lost." After contrasting this order with that in the other passage, he adds the sage comment : " The growth of knowledge and the growth of faith act and react on each other." Sometimes in both Gospel and Epistle the verb " to know " is used where it might seem that " to believe " would convey the same meaning. The one clear distinction that can be pointed out is that though St. John never says that Jesus has faith in God, in at least four passages [2] it is said that he has seen, or has knowledge of, God.

The unusually frequent use of the verb γινώσκειν in the Johannine Gospel and Epistles is no doubt due to the Gnostic atmosphere in which the author lived and worked. His purpose was probably to set forth Christianity as the true *Gnosis* while exposing the unsoundness of much that prided itself upon that pretentious name. When he wrote in allusion to the antichrists who had gone out of the Church with their spurious teaching, " Ye have an anointing from the Holy One, and all know," [3] he expressed the view that this much vaunted γνῶσις, which a little coterie regarded as their monopoly, cannot be compared with the illumination of the Spirit whose gifts are for every member of the Church. In the same way the Johan-

---

[1] *I.C.C.*, Johannine Epistles, p. 122.

[2] John vii. 9 ; viii. 55 ; x. 15 ; xvii. 25.

[3] 1 John ii. 20. The reading καὶ οἴδατε πάντες is undoubtedly original ; πάντα is an easy correction which misses the point.

nine Christ is represented as saying to those who had
believed him: " If ye abide in my word, then are ye
truly my disciples ; and ye shall know the truth, and
the truth shall make you free." [1] In an earlier lecture [2]
we saw how those words fit into the context of a
rabbinic argument. But to the readers of the Gospel
they might well carry a further meaning, for one of the
Gnostic conceptions was that γνῶσις conferred on
those who received it ἐξουσία, " authority," which
freed them from εἱμαρμένη, " destiny." Whereas the
freedom of which Jesus spoke was deliverance from
the bondage of sin.

Another contemporary tendency was to regard
γνῶσις as the result of a purely intellectual process.
Thus Philo taught that in intercourse with God the
stage of faith can be left behind when man reaches the
summit of ἐπιστήμη, " science," which is just γνῶσις.
So in the Hermetic writings, " knowledge is the per-
fection of science, and science is the gift of God." [3]
We learn from the Pauline letters that many years
before the Johannine writings a false pride of intellect
was the besetting sin of many in the Corinthian
Church. They had to be reminded that " knowledge
puffs up, but love builds up." [4] The same over-
weening confidence in the range of man's unaided
powers to soar to the heights of divine being and
to sound the depths of the wisdom of God led St.

---

[1] John viii. 31f.   [2] See pp. 87–92.
[3] Cf. W. Bauer, Handb. z. NT., Das Johannes-Evangelium [3], p. 104.
See Philo, Migr. Abr. 175. Cf. Quod Deus, 143, τὸ δὲ τέρμα τῆς ὁδοῦ γνῶσίς
ἐστι καὶ ἐπιστήμη θεοῦ. Corp. Herm. x. 10a, γνῶσις δέ ἐστιν ἐπιστήμης
τὸ τέλος, ἐπιστήμη δὲ δῶρον τοῦ θεοῦ. W. Scott (Hermetica, ii. p. 247),
however, thinks the reference to ἐπιστήμη has passed into the text from a
marginal note.
[4] 1 Cor. viii. 1, ἡ γνῶσις φυσιοῖ, ἡ δὲ ἀγάπη οἰκοδομεῖ.

John to utter his unmistakable warning against a false *Gnosis*.[1]

Just as faith is morally conditioned, so also knowledge of divine things requires a certain spiritual fitness and is subject to tests which are laid down with great plainness of speech in the First Epistle. In the Gospel the challenge is thrown down: "How can ye believe, which receive glory one of another, and the glory which cometh from the only God ye seek not ? "[2] So also without the right temper of soul knowledge to discern the divine origin of the teaching of Christ is out of reach. "If any man willeth to do his will, he shall know of the teaching, whether it is of God, or whether I speak from myself."[3] Conduct and character determine the validity of the claim to knowledge. "He that saith I know him, and keepeth not his commandments, is a liar, and the truth is not in him."[4] "Whosoever sinneth hath not seen him, neither knoweth him."[5] The peril of the false *Gnosis* lay partly in a facile claim to a knowledge which can only be reached by the disciplined life of obedience to the divine commands, and partly in a mystical pietism which avoided the obligations of the brotherhood.

In the Gospel according to St. Mark the story is told of a rich man who came to Jesus asking what he must do to inherit eternal life. His conventional use of the word " good " induced the question, " Why

---

[1] In contrast with this pride of knowledge Paul sacrificed every privilege " to know Christ in the power of his resurrection and the fellowship of his sufferings " (Phil. iii. 10). " The basis of a genuine heart-to-heart knowledge of Christ is His risen life. The later development in the Johannine literature is the elaboration of Paul's position : ' He who possesses the Son possesses life ' (1 John v. 12)." H. A. A. Kennedy, *Theology of the Epistles*, p. 70.

[2] John v. 44.   [3] John vii. 17.   [4] 1 John ii. 4.   [5] 1 John iii. 6.

callest thou me good? none is good save one, even
God." [1]   In other words, the quest of eternal life is
the search for goodness, god-likeness, and so for the
knowledge of God. Jesus then told the inquirer to
keep the commandments. But those which he selected
for special attention are those which deal not with
man's duty to God, but with his duty to man. " Do
not kill, Do not commit adultery, Do not steal, Do not
bear false witness, Do not defraud, Honour thy father
and mother." The Jesus of the Fourth Gospel declares :
" This is life eternal, to be coming to know thee, the
only true God, and him whom thou hast sent." [2]
The First Epistle tells us that such knowledge is given
only to those who keep the royal command of Christ.
" If a man say, I love God, and hateth his brother, he
is a liar : for he that loveth not his brother whom he
hath seen, cannot love God whom he hath not seen." [3]

Faith and knowledge are closely related, but without
Love union with God—fellowship with Christ—is
beyond our reach. Forty years earlier St. Paul had
written to the Corinthians that " to know all mysteries and all *gnosis*," and to have mountain-moving
faith, is futile in the absence of love.[4] The reason
for this is set forth in this First Epistle. It is rooted in
the nature of God himself. God is love. Knowledge
of God depends upon moral affinity with him.[5] The
Johannine ethic is based upon the Johannine theology.
Love is not a kindly sentiment of vague good-will, nor
is it a genial affability. The Jewish strain in the writer
is shown by the emphasis laid upon will and action
in his use of the word. " Thou shalt love thy neighbour
as thyself " had never been an appeal to the emotions

---

[1] Mark x. 17ff.   [2] John xvii. 3.   [3] 1 John iv. 20.   [4] 1 Cor. xiii. 2.
[5] *Cf.* J. R. Illingworth, *Personality Human and Divine*, Lecture V.

but to the practical effort to place the interest of others on the same plane as the instinct of self-interest. But this is now raised to a far higher level. For love in the Christian disciple is a response to the love of God revealed to us in the sacrifice of his Son.[1] Just as faith is the human response to grace, so love in the heart of man is the answer awakened by divine love, and shown in love of the brethren.

Again we notice how remote the teaching on this subject is from mere speculation about the divine nature. As Dr. Moffatt has said : [2] "'God is love' is not the clue to the origin of the world, but to the moral bliss of man. John is not thinking of a pervasive love-principle in the universe." Nor, as he points out in another place,[3] is the love-relation between the Father and the Son "a detached piece of celestial speculation, like some of the gnostic elaborations of a tie between heavenly aeons. The love of Father and Son is bound up with the mission and message of God's love to the world of men ; the significance of it is missed when it is detached and isolated."

The love of God is seen in the unity of the divine life : "I and my Father are one." [4] So this unity is revealed in a unity of redemptive purpose : "Therefore doth the Father love me, because I lay down my life." [5] This is at one with the love of God for the world in giving his only Son to save it. In response to this love of God for us our love goes out to God, and then to our brethren. "We love because he first loved us." [6]

---

[1] For the interchange of faith and love as the organ of recognition in St. John, see Bultmann, *op. cit.* pp. 113, n. 5, 201, 239. The active force of ἀγαπᾶν "to prefer," "to decide for," is clear in John iii. 19 ; xii. 43 ; xiv. 15, 21ff., as of φιλεῖν in xvi. 27.   [2] *Love in the N.T.*, p. 253.

[3] *Ib.* p. 259.   [4] John x. 30 ; *cf.* xvii. 20–6.   [5] John x. 17.

[6] 1 John iv. 19.

F2

" Hereby know we love, because he laid down his life for us : and we ought to lay down our lives for the brethren." [1]   But as this may seem too remote a demand, to guard us against sentimental heroism the practical nature of love is again insisted upon : " But whoso hath this world's goods, and beholdeth his brother in need, and shutteth up his compassion from him, how doth the love of God abide in him ? My little children, let us not love in word, neither with the tongue ; but in deed and truth." [2]   There are places where we feel that St. John is limiting his outlook to the narrow circle of the Christian brotherhood, with some indifference to the wider claims of society as a whole. The answer to this implied criticism is partly that he regards the Christian brotherhood as the school in which the Christian character is trained. Moreover, the words just quoted seem to carry us into a wider field of action. If man's love to man is determined by God's love to man, then, as that is universal in its scope, so also will the limitless claims of human need enlarge yet more and more the scope of this inspired activity of love.

Faith, knowledge, love—these three are aspects of the approach of man to God, by which union with God is attained.

In closing, let us compare three writers, Philo, St. Paul, and St. John, in their treatment of the concentration of purpose needful to reach this goal, and of the confident mood which it inspires.

Reference has already been made to Philo's emphasis upon the intellectual factor in faith. [3]   Yet nowhere does he disclose a more glowing religious enthusiasm than in his discussion of the faith of Abraham. So he

---

[1] 1 John iii. 16.   [2] 1 John iii. 17t.   [3] See p. 166.

declares : " In what else are we to put our faith (save in God) ?   In leadership or reputations or honours, or in abundance of wealth and noble birth, or in health and quick sensibility, or in bodily strength and beauty ? . . . Faith towards God is the only true and steadfast good. So that one may say with utmost truth that he who has put his faith in the former things distrusts God, while he who distrusts them has put his faith in God." [1] We may compare with this St. Paul's : " But what things were gain to me, these I count as loss for Christ's sake. Nay, I count all things as loss in comparison with the surpassing worth of knowing Christ Jesus my Lord, that I may gain Christ, and be found at the end in him." [2]   The Johannine parallel is instructive. " Love not the world, neither the things that are in the world. If any man love the world, the love of the Father is not in him. For all that is in the world, the lust of the flesh, the lust of the eyes, and the vainglory of life, is not of the Father, but is of the world. And the world passeth away and the lust thereof; but he that doeth the will of God abideth for ever." [3]

One of the most characteristic words in the vocabulary of early Christianity is παρρησία. Originally meaning " readiness to say anything," it came to mean that confidence in which perfect candour is possible. Philo rises to impassioned eloquence when describing this " glad fearlessness of bearing." [4]   Of Moses he writes : " The noble man exercises such παρρησία that he dares not only to speak and shout, but actually as the outcome of pure trust and genuine emotion to cry

---

[1] *Abr.* 263, 268f.   [2] Phil. iii. 7, 8.   [3] 1 John ii. 15–7.
[4] So H. A. A. Kennedy paraphrases this expressive word.   See *Philo's Contribution to Religion*, p. 129, a book to which this writer owes his first interest in Philo.

out in reproach." [1] " Παρρησία is akin to friendship. For to whom should a man speak with frankness but to his friend ? And so most excellent is it, that in the oracles Moses is proclaimed as the friend of God to show that all the audacities of his bold discourse were uttered in friendship, rather than in presumption." [2] Or again, Abraham, the father of the men of faith, is made to say : " What was I that thou shouldst impart speech to me, that thou shouldst promise me for a reward a boon more complete than a gift or a bounty. Am not I an exile from my homeland, an outcast from my kinsfolk, an alien from my father's house ? But thou, O Lord, art to me my homeland, thou art my kinsfolk, . . . thou art my reward, my παρρησία. . . . Why then should I not dare to utter my thoughts ? Yet I who speak of daring confess my fear and consternation. . . . Without ceasing, therefore, I am continuing to enjoy this blending of good things, which has induced me neither to speak boldly without godly fear, nor to show godly fear without boldness of speech." [3]

With St. Paul the everlasting wonder is that through Jesus Christ he has learnt to cry " Abba, Father," and to breathe the very spirit of sonship. One of the effects of this reception into sonship is παρρησία. " To me who am less than the least of all saints was this grace given, to preach to the Gentiles the unsearchable riches of Christ, and to make known what is the dispensation of the mystery hidden from eternity in God who created all things, that now to the principalities and the powers in the heavenly places might be made known through the Church the manifold wisdom of God, according to the eternal purpose which he

---

[1] *Quis Rer. Div.*, 19.   [2] *Ib.* 21.   [3] *Ib.* 26, 29.

purposed in Christ Jesus our Lord, in whom we have παρρησία and access in confidence through faith in him." [1]

After this the language of St. John is simple. " Beloved, if our heart condemn us not, we have παρρησία before God." [2] " Herein has love been made perfect with us, that we may have παρρησία in the day of judgement, for even as he is, so are we in this world. There is no fear in love, but perfect love casteth out fear, for fear hath torment, and he who feareth is not made perfect in love." [3]

And so the last advent and the dark betrayal night are brought together. The glad fearlessness which is the gift of the spirit of Christ is the expression of the new relationship which was first declared in the gracious words : " You are my friends if you do the things which I command you. No longer do I call you servants . . ., but friends." [4]

---

[1] Eph. iii. 8-12.   [2] 1 John iii. 21.   [3] 1 John iv. 17f.
[4] John xv. 14f. *Cf.* Wisd. vii. 27f. (upon which J. A. F. Gregg's notes are excellent) :

> From generation to generation passing into holy souls
> She maketh men friends of God and prophets.
> For nothing doth God love save him that dwelleth with wisdom.

CHAPTER VIII

THE WAY, THE TRUTH, AND THE LIFE

THE earliest name by which the Christian Church was
known to its opponents was The Way. When Saul,
" breathing threatening and slaughter against the
disciples of the Lord," went to the high priest for
letters to the synagogue of Damascus, it was that " if
he found any that were of the Way, he might bring
them bound to Jerusalem." [1] The apostle Paul's
secession from the synagogue at Ephesus took place
" when some were hardened and disobedient, speaking
evil of the Way before the multitude." [2] The riot of
Demetrius and his fellow-craftsmen at Ephesus is
described by Luke after the introductory remark that
"about that time there arose no small stir concerning the
Way." [3] In his defence before Felix Paul confesses "that
after the Way which they call a sect, so serve I the God
of our fathers." [4] And at the close of his speech Felix,
" having more exact knowledge concerning the Way," [5]
deferred judgement until the arrival of Claudius Lysias.
The term may have been chosen by their Jewish
neighbours in Jerusalem, because the word was often
heard on the lips of the disciples themselves. They
were following a new way of life, their manner of
fellowship marked them out from their fellow members

[1] Acts ix. 1f.   [2] Ib. xix. 9.   [3] Ib. xix. 23.
[4] Ib. xxiv. 14.   [5] Ib. xxiv. 22.

of the synagogue, or from those whom they met daily in the temple.

The metaphor has played its part more than once in the history of religion. The Buddhist Way of Happiness was the Noble Eightfold Path. The two older religions of China were rival interpretations of the doctrine of Tao, " the Way," Confucius on the whole giving it a moral and Lao-Tse a metaphysical meaning.

There is a well-known passage in which Philo writes about the Way. " The king's way then, which we have just said to be true and genuine philosophy, is called in the Law the utterance and word of God. For it is written, ' Thou shalt not swerve aside from the word which I command thee this day to the right hand nor to the left hand ' (Deut. xxviii. 14). Thus it is clearly proved that the word of God is identical with the king's way. He treats the two as synonymous, and bids us decline from neither, but with upright mind tread the track that leads straight on, a central highway." [1]

It is not likely that this Philonic identification of the royal road with " the study of what is good and fair " has any bearing on this early title given to the primitive Church. That is far more likely to go back to a traditional saying of our Lord, preserved in the Fourth Gospel.[2] It is not impossible that in the circles in which this Gospel took its rise Philo's association of the words ὁδός and λόγος was already known, and that the Evangelist intended his readers to discern a connection between the words in the fourteenth chapter and the summary of the Gospel under the title Logos in the Prologue.

The word " way " is used with many meanings and

---

[1] *Post. Cain.*, 102.   [2] John xiv. 6.

with great frequency in the Old Testament. When it is used of God's ways it stands for his creative activity, for his moral administration, and above all for his commandments. It is enough to recall the 119th Psalm, that long hymn in praise of the Torah, to see how closely this word is allied with such synonyms as "law," "testimonies," "precepts," "statutes," "commandments," "judgements." "Blessed are they that are perfect in the way, Who walk in the law of the Lord." "I will meditate in thy precepts, And have respect unto thy ways. I will delight myself in thy statutes : I will not forget thy word." "I will run the way of thy commandments, When thou shalt enlarge my heart." "Teach me, O Lord, the way of thy statutes : And I shall keep it unto the end." [1] There is yet another use of the figure in the Old Testament to be borne in mind. The purpose of God, foretold by the prophets and fulfilled in Christ, is described as "the way of the Lord" in those passages [2] at the opening of the Gospels where use is made of the *Testimonia* [3] in which Isaiah xl. 3 and Malachi iii. 1 are cited. Accordingly there are two distinct ideas which converge in the Johannine picture of Jesus. He is the fulfilment of the Torah ; he is also the fulfilment of prophecy. He is the new Torah come down from heaven to make known the will of God for men. He is the true and perfect Prophet sent by the Father to make known Him whom no man hath seen nor can see, by declaring : "He that hath seen me hath seen the Father." [4] We have already offered the suggestion that the Transfiguration is represented by anticipation

---

[1] Ps. cxix. 1, 15, 32, 33.   [2] Mark i. 2f. ; Matt. iii. 3 ; Luke iii. 4.
[3] See p. 20.
[4] Ex. xxxiii. 20 ; 1 Tim. vi. 16 ; John v. 37 ; vi. 46 ; xiv. 9.

in the Prologue.[1]   Moses and Elijah, who stand for
Law and Prophecy, according to the Synoptic tradition
met *with* Jesus on the holy mount.   According to St.
John, Moses and Elijah meet *in* Jesus as the Logos,
which is both the Torah and the spoken Word of God.
The same thought which confronts us in the ancient
term, the Way, is here placed upon the lips of Jesus
himself.

" I am the *Way*."   This claim takes the word out of
the category of instruction and sets it in the context
of revelation.   Jesus does not point out the way, nor is
he the guide along the way ; he claims to be himself
the Way.   This does not mean that no ethical demands
are made upon those who enter on discipleship.   It
does mean that the Christian ethic is not a new legalism
but the natural outcome of a new relationship.   In this
respect there is a striking likeness between St. Paul and
St. John.   The Pauline epistles show how bold an
experiment the Apostle to the Gentiles made when he
discarded the Jewish law as an integral part of the
Christian obedience.   There was no small danger that
the raw converts, won from the undisciplined life of
Gentile morals, might degrade liberty into licence.   To
guard against this peril St. Paul emphasized two great
principles : first, that union with Christ imposes an
obligation of consistency ; secondly, that in the life of
the Christian the fruits of the Spirit will appear.   It
has often been urged against Paul that he shows
indifference to the earthly life of Jesus, and that he is
absorbed in the contemplation of the heavenly Christ.
Many recent studies[2] have shown how misleading such

---

[1] See pp. 28f.

[2] *E.g.* C. Anderson Scott, *Living Issues in the N.T.*, ch. i.   *Cf.* also
P. Feine, *Jesus Christus u. Paulus* ; J. Weiss, *Paul and Jesus* ; J. H. Moulton,
" The Gospel according to Paul " (*Expositor*, VIII. ii. pp. 16ff.).

an idea is, for St. Paul constantly harnesses his doctrine
to practical considerations of the moral life. The very
fact that his knowledge of the life and teaching of the
historic Jesus comes out so allusively reminds us that
he could assume on the part of his readers famili-
arity with both the " tradition " (παράδοσις) and the
" teaching " (διδαχή).

This should help us to approach one of the most
perplexing problems raised by the Johannine writings.
Why is it that so little is told us in the Gospel to enable
us to picture the Jesus who stands before us so vividly
in the earlier Gospels ? Why is it that, in letters written
to communities of Christians in the making, there
should be so little to instruct them in the broad outlines
of the Christian character and in the more specific
duties of discipleship ? There is no point at which the
utter inadequacy of Windisch's theory stands more
completely exposed—the theory that St. John's Gospel
was written not to supplement but to supersede the
other Gospels.[1] Without discussing how far the Synoptic Gospels, or any of them, were already known to the
Evangelist, we can confidently assert that by this time
the basic material of the Gospels was part of the common
heritage of the Church. " The things which Jesus
began both to do and to teach " during his earthly
life formed part of the catechetical instruction of those
who were being received into the Church.[2] In writing
his Epistles the Evangelist might well feel that to go
over this ground again would be superfluous, just as
the writer to the Hebrews deprecated a return to the
more elementary Christian doctrine.[3] But how much
lies behind one passing allusion ! " Hereby know we

---

[1] *Johannes u. die Synoptiker*, p. 134.   [2] Luke i. 1-4 ; Acts i. 1.
[3] Heb. vi. 1, διὸ ἀφέντες τὸν τῆς ἀρχῆς τοῦ Χριστοῦ λόγον.

that we are in him : he that saith he abideth in him ought himself also to walk even as he walked." [1] This is a frame, with the legend attached, but where is the picture ? It can hardly be said that it is contained in the Gospel, for there is but one hint there of an example to be followed : " If I then, the Lord and the Master, have washed your feet, ye also ought to wash one another's feet. For I have given you an example, that ye should do as I have done to you." [2] In the Epistle the one commandment is " an old commandment which ye had from the beginning : the old commandment is the word which ye heard." [3] This, we must assume, recalls another word spoken in the upper room: " A new commandment I give unto you, that ye love one another. By this shall all men know that ye are my disciples, if ye have love one to another." [4]

St. Paul's ethical appeal was based upon this note in the teaching of Jesus. For in the very epistle in which he fought most stubbornly for the freedom of the Gentiles from legal bondage he addresses his converts thus : " For ye, brethren, were called for freedom ; only use not your freedom for an occasion to the flesh, but through love be servants one to another. For the whole law is fulfilled in one word, even in this ; Thou shalt love thy neighbour as thyself." [5] In later letters he found it necessary to be more specific. Problems arose which called for the critical judgement of the missionary statesman. Simple people stood in need of the plainest directions about the ordinary relationships of the home. Hence those *Haustafeln* (as the Germans call them) which we find in Colossians and Ephesians,

---

[1] I John ii. 6.   [2] John xiii. 14.   [3] I John ii. 7.
[4] John xiii. 34.   [5] Gal. v. 13ff.

as also in 1 Peter.[1] In course of time two dangers
appeared.   On the one hand, the practical needs of
the Christian Society, separated from the Synagogue
and the moral discipline of the Law, led to the growth
of a new legalism. We see the first traces of this in the
Gospel according to St. Matthew, with its fivefold
arrangement of the teaching of Jesus [2] as the new
Pentateuch.   Such editorial additions as the exceptive
clause in the words about divorce [3] are an indication
of the tendency to codify. As soon as the utterances
of the idealist are translated into the enactments of the
legislator these adjustments and adaptations are necessary. Another example of this legislative tendency may
be seen in the teaching of the Two Ways in the Epistle
of Barnabas and in the *Teaching of the Twelve Apostles*.
Indeed in the *Didache* its most dangerous possibilities
are revealed. " Let not your fasts be with the hypocrites, for they fast on Mondays and Thursdays, but do
you fast on Wednesdays and Fridays. And do not
pray as the hypocrites, but as the Lord commanded in
his Gospel, pray thus." Then after the Lord's Prayer
comes the injunction : " Pray thus three times a day." [4]
How very different from this new legalism is the so-
called *Nomismus* [5] of the Johannine writings ! The
various references to νόμος "law," and ἐντολή, " command," amount to no more than this, that he who lives
in fellowship with Christ must prove the reality of that
union by doing the things which are in harmony with
the Spirit of Christ, and are prompted by love, the
instinct of the soul that is born from above. It is not
the imitation of Jesus which is taught, but a regenerate

---

[1] Col. iii. 18 ; iv. 1 ; Eph. v. 22 ; vi. 9 ; 1 Pet. iii. 1–7.
[2] Matt. v.–vii., x., xiii. 1–52 ; xviii., xxiv.–xxv.   [3] Matt. v. 32 ; xix. 9.
[4] Did. viii.   [5] See H. J. Holtzmann, *Lehrb. d. Nt. Theol.*, ii. p. 434.

life that grows into the likeness of Christ in the fellowship of the redeemed society which is united in
him.

If one danger to be avoided was that of reducing
Christianity to a new legalism, the other, not less
insidious, was that of allowing the Christian ethic to be
undermined by regarding it as independent of the
authority upon which it rests. This danger is met by
emphasizing the function of belief. "And this is his
commandment, that ye should believe in the name of
his Son Jesus Christ, and love one another, even as he
gave us commandment." [1] That is, in Westcott's
words : "Believe as true the message which the name
conveys. The full title, 'His Son Jesus Christ' is a
compressed creed." [2] Any teaching which denied the
reality of the Incarnation, either by relieving the Son
of God of the actual suffering of the sacrifice of love
upon the cross, or else by refusing to him the relationship which alone gives validity to his claim to reveal
the Father, is ultimately destructive of the Christian
way of life. "This is the antichrist, even he that
denieth the Father and the Son, Whosoever denieth
the Son, the same hath not the Father : he that con-
fesseth the Son hath the Father also." [3]

This brings us back to the great affirmation: "I am
the way. No man cometh unto the Father but by
me." This is the theme of the Gospel. It underlies all
the teaching of the Epistles. The words are not to be
understood as a disparagement of all the soaring
imaginations of seekers after God in any age or race
of men. Still less should we read into them a repudia-
tion of all that had been spoken by prophetic seers in

[1] 1 John iii. 23.   [2] *The Epistles of St. John*, p. 120.
[3] 1 John ii. 22-23.

their fragmentary witness to Israel. Many had sought God, and had been found by Him. The uniqueness of the revelation in Christ is that in him we have the Way to the *Father*. By the secret of his perfect filial consciousness he brings us through his renewing Spirit into fellowship with the Father. " I and the Father are one." " I pray for those whom thou hast given me." " I pray for them also that believe on me through their word ; that they may all be one ; even as thou, Father, art in me, and I in thee, that they also may be in us." [1]

This self-designation of Jesus as the Way was an answer to Thomas's question, " Lord, we know not whither thou goest ; how know we the way ? " Some have felt that the claim of Jesus to be the Truth and the Life are irrelevant to this question, and John Lightfoot,[2] the seventeenth-century rabbinic scholar, made the suggestion that " I am the way, and the truth, and the life " may be a Hebrew idiom, according to which the added noun has an adjectival force. Thus Jeremiah xxix. 11 : " To give you an end and expectation " means " to give you an expected end," or as Kimchi explains it : " A good end even as you expect." So " the way, and the truth, and the life " may be a Semitic idiom for " the true and living way," and this is the rendering which Moffatt gives in his *New Translation of the New Testament*. It serves to emphasize the word which is explained in the next clause. It also suggests a comparison with some words in the Epistle to the Hebrews : " Having therefore, brethren, boldness to enter into the holy place by the blood of Jesus, by the way which he dedicated for us, a new and

[1] John x. 30 ; xvii. 9, 20f.
[2] *Horae Hebraicae* (Oxford, 1859), iii. p. 398.

living way, . . . let us draw near with a true heart in fulness of faith." [1]   But it is unnecessary to limit the phrase in this way. Truth and Life are both key words in the Johannine message of Christianity.

" *Truth* " is associated with " way " several times in the Psalter. " Teach me thy way, O Lord : I will walk in thy truth " ; " I have walked in thy truth " ; " All the paths of the Lord are lovingkindness and truth Unto such as keep his covenant and his testimonies." [2]   It should be observed, however, that the word ἀλήθεια, which is so frequent in the New Testament and especially in the Johannine writings, is a word which derives its meaning in early Christian use partly from its Old Testament equivalent ʾ*meth*, and partly from its history in the various stages of the Greek language. The Hebrew word has rather the meaning of " faithfulness," " trustworthiness," " permanence," " sureness," whereas in Greek ἀλήθεια has the meaning of " truth " as opposed to " falsehood," or of " reality " as opposed to mere appearance.

In the Gospel and Epistles of John the word " truth " is first the standard of knowledge and of utterance and then the standard of action. There can be no discord between knowing and doing. Further, the Truth is God's gift to men, and as God's presence in men it unites man with God. This applies not only to religious truth but to truth in a more general sense. In so far as men are of the truth they are of God. The religious life, in the Johannine view, largely revolves round the truth. Truth is set forth insistently as man's need and at the same time his duty. Truth sets men free. Truth is the characteristic of the Spirit. Truth

[1] Heb. x. 19f.   [2] Ps. lxxxvi. 11 ; xxvi. 3 ; xxv. 10.

is a living power sent forth from God, and St. John does not hesitate to identify both Jesus and the Spirit with the Truth.

How far is St. John influenced by the Old Testament or by the Jewish idea of Truth, and how far by its Hellenistic connotation ?   Generally speaking, we find little trace of the original Hebrew meaning of " faithfulness." Ἀλήθεια is used far more in its characteristically Greek sense.   This does not mean that the Johannine word and thought are independent of the Jewish usage and are employed simply in accordance with contemporary Hellenistic ideas.   The word had undergone considerable modification as a result of the impact of Greek thought upon Judaism.[1]   Some of the expressions used by St. John bear traces of this Old Testament association.   Thus, in the earliest use of the word in the Gospel, the Logos is spoken of twice over in a descriptive phrase borrowed from the account of the law-giving in Exodus : "Jehovah, a God of compassion and gracious, slow to anger, and plenteous in mercy and truth." [2]   The LXX translated that last phrase πολυέλεος καὶ ἀληθινός, but the phrase in John, "full of grace and truth," is far nearer to the Hebrew idiom, even though the characteristic Hebrew word for " mercy " or " lovingkindness " is replaced by the distinctively Christian, but not Johannine, word for " grace."   Then again, a few verses later, the Logos, the new Torah, unlike that given on Sinai, " came as grace and truth" in Jesus Christ.   In this connection it is interesting to find that in the Midrash of Psalm xxv. it is said that the Torah, as the expression of the divine word and the divine being, is therefore at the same

---

[1] Cf. Dan. viii. 12, " It cast down truth to the ground," where " truth " means " the true religion."   [2] Ex. xxxiv. 6.

time *'emeth*. This thought of the divine *'emeth* or " truth " finds its most powerful symbolic expression in rabbinical exposition in the figure of God's seal. Thus " God's seal is *'emeth*. What does *'emeth* mean ? That He, God, lives, and is everlasting King." [1] There are two passages in the Gospel where this symbol occurs. The first is in the second part of the conversation with Nicodemus (iii. 31–36). It must be quoted in its context because of the light it throws on the Prologue. " He that cometh from above is above all : he that is of the earth is of the earth, and of the earth he speaketh : he that cometh from heaven is above all. What he hath seen and heard, of that he beareth witness ; and no man receiveth his witness. He that hath received his witness hath set his seal to this that God is true. For he whom God hath sent speaketh the words of God : for he giveth not the Spirit by measure." The second is in the discourse on the Bread of Life. " Work not for the meat which perisheth, but for the meat which abideth unto eternal life, which the Son of Man shall give unto you : for him the Father, even God, hath sealed." [2] These passages show the Jewish colouring of the Johannine language. But the word " truth " has its Greek meaning of " reality." The message is that " the reality of God's nature is gracious." [3] The self-communicating divine life has actually come to men in Jesus Christ. From that life of God which alone has reality and permanence an activity of love has entered into the plane of history and brought the gift of eternal life into the present. Truth is not a correct conception of God to be apprehended by the intellect so much

---

[1] See G. Kittel, art. ἀλήθεια, *Theol. Wörterb. z. N.T.*, i. p. 238.
[2] John vi. 27.   [3] Moffatt, *Grace in the N.T.*, p. 367.

as a revelation of reality to be received in a personal relationship.[1]

On the human side, knowledge of the truth is both active and passive. Passive in so far as it is God who reveals, and man the recipient of grace who receives his revelation ; active because the coming of light into the world demands that we " come to the light," and " walk in the light," and that we put into practice what he has revealed. In this connection we observe the Johannine use of the Hebrew phrase " to do the truth." " He that doeth the truth cometh to the light, that his works may be made manifest that they have been wrought in God." [2]   " If we say that we have fellow-ship with him and walk in the darkness, we lie, and do not the truth ; but if we walk in the light, as he is in the light, we have fellowship with one another, and the blood of Jesus his Son cleanseth us from all sin." [3] The same blending of active and passive appears in the great prayer : " Consecrate them in the truth ; thy word is truth. . . . And for their sakes I consecrate myself that they also may be consecrated in truth." [4] But it is also said : " They have kept thy word," [5] that is, " They have kept thy truth." The loyalty of the disciples, who had remained steadfast when many others turned their backs on Christ, was shown by their recognition that he had words of eternal life, and was the Holy One of God. [6] That disclosure of the divine will was now to reach its climax. Sacrificial

---

[1] Yet note the one use of διάνοια by St. John (1 John v. 20) and G. G. Findlay's comment (op. cit. p. 427) : " [His] creed is that of the sound intellect as well as of the simple heart. . . . St. John has done well to tell us that διάνοια no less than πνεῦμα and ἀγάπη is the gift of Christ."

[2] John iii. 21.   [3] 1 John i. 6, 7.   [4] John xvii. 17, 19.
[5] John xvii. 6.   [6] John vi. 66ff.

language is rare in this Gospel, though not quite so rare in the First Epistle. When it is found it is not developed but is allusive. This prayer was offered on the eve of the crucifixion. Possibly the Epistle to the Hebrews, which in many respects shows an outlook similar to that of St. John, helps us to expand the terse clause just quoted. After citing the words, " Lo, I come to do thy will," in contrast to the sacrifices of the Old Covenant, the writer continues, " And by this will we have been consecrated through the offering of the body of Jesus Christ once for all." [1] When, by this self-offering of Christ upon the cross, the disciples have been fully consecrated to their new mission of witnessing to the world the revelation of the Incarnate Life, they will be under the guidance of the Spirit of truth. This new condition will not consist in a vague spirituality, but will be a further progress along the way by which they have hitherto been led. In the words of F. J. A. Hort : " the knowledge of Christ as the Truth shall constitute the substance of all their future learning, while the Spirit of the Truth shall train and enlighten them in the perception and application of it." [2] With this confidence in the Christian Gospel as a revelation in time of ultimate reality, St. John grapples in his First Epistle with the false guides who would substitute an unsubstantial shadow for the historic foundation of the Faith. Thus his dissertation reaches its climax in those triumphant certainties closing with the words : " We know that the Son of God is come, and hath given us an understanding, that we know him that is true, and we are in him that is true, even in his Son Jesus Christ. This

---

[1] Heb. x. 10.   [2] *The Way, the Truth and the Life*, p. 58.

is the true God and eternal life. My little children, guard yourselves from idols." [1]

These words give us the necessary transition to the third great keyword, *Life*. Eternal life stands in closest relation to the apprehension of that which is true through fellowship with " him who is true." In the Gospel eternal life is described as gaining knowledge of the only true God and of Jesus Christ whom he " sent." [2] The connection between life and truth is a recurrent theme in the Johannine writings. Two corresponding adjectives are used, ἀληθής and ἀληθινός, and though sometimes the distinction in meaning is not strictly observed, on the whole it may be said that ἀληθής is the Latin *verax*, and ἀληθινός the Latin *verus*, so that Trench's well-known epigram holds good : The ἀληθής fulfils the promise of his lips, the ἀληθινός fulfils the wider promise of his name.[3] Statistics are sometimes of use in testing the characteristic thought of a writer. Ἀληθής is used thirteen times in the Johannine Gospel, twice in the Epistles, and nine times in all the rest of the New Testament. Ἀληθινός is used once by Luke, once by Paul, six times in the Apocalypse in addition to three times when it clearly means the same as ἀληθής. But it is used eleven times in St. John's Gospel and First Epistle, and three times in Hebrews, which here again shows affinity with Johannine thought. Just as " the true tabernacle "

[1] 1 John v. 20f. Ὁ ἀληθινός and ὁ ἀληθινὸς θεός must refer to the Father, not to the Son. (See the commentaries by Westcott, Brooke, Baumgarten, and Windisch.) " The God who completely fulfils the highest conceptions of Godhead is the God who has been revealed in Jesus Christ, as contrasted with all false conceptions of God, against which the readers are warned in the next verse" (A. E. Brooke, *op. cit.* p. 152.)   [2] John xvii. 3.

[3] *Synonyms of the N.T.* (New Edition, 1901), p. 28.

in Hebrews [1] is the heavenly reality of which the earthly structure is but an imperfect copy, so the " true light," " the true bread," " the true vine " are " things that verify their names, realities behind the appearance." [2]

The starting-point for a study of the connection between this conception of " truth " and that of " life " in the Johannine thought is the discourse on the Bread of Life in the sixth chapter of the Gospel. It is said that in contrast to the manna in the wilderness, " My Father giveth you the real bread from heaven. For the bread of God is that which cometh down out of heaven, and giveth life unto the world." " I am the bread of life." " This is the bread which cometh down out of heaven, that a man may eat thereof and not die." " I am the living bread which came down out of heaven : if a man eat of this bread, he shall live for ever : yea and the bread which I will give is my flesh for the life of the world." " He that eateth my flesh and drinketh my blood abideth in me, and I in him. As the living Father sent me, and I live because of the Father : so he that eateth me, he also shall live because of me." [3] Here it is to be observed that " the real bread " is " the bread of life," that it " comes down from heaven," that " the living bread " is Jesus himself, who gives his mortal life, his life in the flesh, to give life to the world. But we also observe that with this conception of eternal life as something conferred now on those who accept it in Christ, there is a promise of being " raised at the last day." [4]

---

[1] Heb. viii. 2.
[2] G. G. Findlay, *Fellowship in the Life Eternal*, p. 428.
[3] John vi. 32, 35, 48, 50f., 56f.   [4] John vi. 54.

It is clear that we have here a line of thought which is expressed in an idiom quite different from that which we find in the Synoptic Gospels, and it would be wrong to preclude the possibility that the Johannine presentation owes something to the religious currency of the Hellenistic world.[1] But too often it has been taken for granted that we have here a complete break with Palestinian Christianity and a transformation of the teaching of Jesus into a Hellenistic religion. The evidence given by Strack and Billerbeck [2] shows that the term " eternal life " corresponds to Jewish formulae, Hebrew and Aramaic, and we know from the Synoptic Gospels that it was sometimes used by Jesus or those who addressed him as equivalent to " the kingdom of God." Friedrich Büchsel has shown that the term ζωὴ αἰώνιος is very rare in Philo, indeed, according to Leisegang's Index to Philo, the expression is actually found but once, and it is only rarely that the parallel phrases, ζωὴ ἀθάνατος, ζωὴ ἀΐδιος, ζωὴ ἄφθαρτος are found. In the Hermetic writings ζωή often occurs, but the cosmological-metaphysical aspect which so often attaches to it is quite un-Johannine, and the religious use is not identical. The common feature of the two conceptions is that " life comes to man from God, and through a spiritual revelation of God, which at the same time creates an entirely new man." [3]

The word αἰώνιος takes us back to Plato, with the meaning of " pertaining to an aeon," that is, a life-

[1] See Additional Note D, p. 204.
[2] *Op. cit.* i. pp. 267, 808, 829 ; iii. pp. 129ff. Observe the passages cited in ii. p. 467, and in Schlatter, *Der Evangelist Johannes*, pp. 158ff., for the gift of eternal life in the Torah.
[3] *Johannes u. d. hellenistische Synkretismus*, p. 55, n.[1], p. 57.

time, or an epoch.[1]   But in the words of Professor
John Baillie : " Plato uses it to denote that which has
neither beginning nor end and is subject to neither
change nor decay—that which is above time, but of
which time is a moving image." [2]   Now the New
Testament usage of the phrase has the meaning,
" pertaining to a particular age," to the age of messianic expectation.   This gives the term its qualitative
sense, though of course there is also a quantitative
connotation.   St. John is in line with the Pauline
teaching, " to be spiritually minded is life," [3] when he
says of the Logos, " in him was life," or of Jesus, " I
came that they might have life, and have it abundantly." [4]

In an earlier lecture [5] we have considered the way
in which the Johannine teaching of eternal life is
related to some of the sayings in the Synoptic Gospels
where the " powers of the age to come," that is, of the
kingdom of God, are already regarded as present.
Professor C. H. Dodd has suggested a fuller connection
between the older eschatology and the outlook of this
Evangelist.   " This eternal order is the Kingdom of
God into which Christians have been born again, by
water and the Spirit (iii. 3–8).   That is to say, life is
for them fully real ; they are nurtured by the *real*

---

[1] Moulton-Milligan, *Vocabulary*, p. 16, *s.v.* αἰώνιος, note that outside
the N.T., in the vernacular as in the classical Greek, it never loses the
sense of *perpetuus*.   " In general, the word depicts that of which the
horizon is not in view, whether the horizon be at an infinite distance,
as in Catullus's poignant lines :

> Nobis cum semel occidit brevis lux,
> Nox est *perpetua* una dormienda,

or whether it lies no farther than the span of a Caesar's life."

[2] *And the Life Everlasting*, p. 206.

[3] Rom. viii. 6 : τὸ φρόνημα τοῦ πνεύματος ζωὴ καὶ εἰρήνη.

[4] John i. 4 ; x. 10.   [5] Lect. V., p. 117.

bread, and abide in the *real* Vine. This is the Johannine equivalent for the primitive Christian declaration that the age of fulfilment has dawned, or the Pauline declaration that if any man is in Christ there is a new creation. Its organic relation to primitive eschatological conceptions can be illustrated in various ways." [1]

Christianity according to St. John is a revelation of the glory of God in the historic life of Jesus, in whom we find the Way, the Truth, and the Life. But he also sees that glory displayed to the believing eyes of those who know the Risen Christ in the life eternal which is the Fellowship of the Spirit. To him the past, the present, and the future are fused into one life; the life of the Incarnate Word, the life eternal of the disciple in the community of the faithful controlled and inspired by the Spirit, and the perfected life when Christ shall have been manifested and we shall see him as he is.

---

[1] *The Apostolic Preaching and its Developments*, pp. 157f. The illustrations are most illuminating.

EPILOGUE

On a bright June morning in the year 1915 two
travellers in the English Lakes started early from the
little village of Mardale and climbed the steep ascent
of Kidsty Pike. On reaching the summit they flung
themselves down to recover breath and to gaze upon
range after range of Lakeland hills. Amid the solitude
of those peaceful fells it was hard to think of the
anguish of war that was desolating north-eastern
France and Flanders. Then suddenly another scene
unfolded itself against the present background. According to the map the nearest ridge bore the strange name
of High Street, and it was not difficult to discern the
remains of the old Roman road that once ran along the
topmost line. In a moment the drone of innumerable
insects and the confused murmur of sounds from the
village far below were changed into the sound of the
tramp of many feet. The sunlight caught the glint
of helmet and spear-point. A detachment of legionaries
was on the march from the castle on the Lune to
Hadrian's wall 'twixt Tyne and Solway Firth. We
were on the most distant fringe of Empire. Jungle and
bog and weald might cover the greater part of this
island of Britain. Yet we were linked to the city of
the seven hills, and through her to the furthermost
reaches of her far-flung dominion by one bond—the
Road. All roads led to Rome. The sun might hide
himself behind thick clouds. Dense mists might blot

G   193

out all the landscape, yet if we did but follow that road in the right direction it would bring us at last to a harbour on the southern coast. There we should find a boat to carry us across the channel to a haven on the coast of Gaul, and then, by following another road, in spite of all the perils of the way we might hope at last to arrive at the eternal city, the heart of empire. That road is the symbol of unity amidst all the bewildering variety of peoples and tribes and tongues, and the perplexing obstruction of forest and mountain and stream. The road is the pledge of purpose and of power. Which things are a parable.

Nearly seventy years ago Dr. F. J. A. Hort delivered the Hulsean Lectures which were published more than twenty years later under the title *The Way the Truth the Life*. In that profoundest treatment which these words have ever received they are said to be " the practical and ethical expression of an all-embracing truth which we may perhaps apprehend best in the form of two separate doctrines : first, that the whole seeming maze of history in nature and man, the tumultuous movement of the world in progress, has running through it one supreme dominating Way ; and second, that He who on earth was called Jesus the Nazarene *is* that Way." [1]

Some five hundred years ago an " old Dutch monk in his white-washed cell " meditated on these words. Let us close our study of Christianity according to St. John by recalling this page from Thomas a Kempis. [2]

" Follow thou me. I am the Way the Truth and the Life. Without the Way there is no going ; without the Truth there is no knowing : without the Life there is no living. I am the Way which thou must follow ;

[1] *Op. cit.* pp. 20f.   [2] *The Imitation of Christ*, Chap. LVI. i.

the Truth which thou must believe : the Life which thou must hope for.

"I am the inviolable Way; the infallible Truth : the never-ending Life. I am the straightest Way ; the sovereign Truth : Life true Life blessed Life uncreated. If thou remain in My way thou shalt know the Truth ; and the Truth shall make thee free : and thou shalt lay hold on eternal Life."

ADDITIONAL NOTES

NOTE A

The Johannine outlook Judaic rather than Hellenistic

Hans Pribnow has contributed a useful reminder to this discussion. In *Die johanneische Anschauung vom " Leben "* (1934), pp. 16f., he points out that a whole group of terms are missing in the Johannine writings which are exceedingly common in the contemporary religious literature of the Hellenistic world, and which might seem to come inevitably into the vocabulary of a writer whose cardinal conception is " Life." The words are ἀθανασία and ἀθάνατος, ἀφθαρσία and ἄφθαρτος.

These words play their part in the Mystery cults, and in the kind of mysticism which is independent of ritual, as in the *Corpus Hermeticum* i. 18, 28 ; x. 4f. ; xiii. 3 (Scott, i. pp. 124, 132, 188f., 240). References to Philo will be found in Leisegang's Index to Cohn and Wendland's edition of the Greek text. How far this language has penetrated the Judaism of the Diaspora can also be seen in the *Wisdom of Solomon* (ii. 23 ; iii. 1f. ; iv. 1 ; vi. 19 ; viii. 13, 17 ; xv. 3) and in 4 Maccabees (xiv. 5f. ; xvi. 13 ; xviii. 23).

Pribnow concludes that St. John has deliberately avoided using these terms because for his readers they would have conveyed a meaning which was out of harmony with his eschatology.

" *Birth from above.*" " *Begotten of God.*"

" Regeneration " is a conception which appears in
several writings in the N.T., with the use of a variety
of descriptive terms.

In the Johannine writings the terms are γεννηθῆναι
(γεγέννησθαι) ἄνωθεν, ἐξ ὕδατος καὶ πνεύματος, ἐκ τοῦ
πνεύματος (John iii. 3, 5, 8), ἐξ αὐτοῦ, ἐκ τοῦ θεοῦ
(1 John ii. 29 ; iii, 9 ; iv. 7 ; v. 1, 4, 18). In James i. 18
the expression is different : βουληθεὶς ἀπεκύησεν ἡμᾶς
λόγῳ ἀληθείας. In 1 Peter the verb ἀναγεννᾶν (ἀναγε-
γέννησθαι) is used (i. 3, 23). Another word appears
in Titus iii. 5 : ἔσωσεν ἡμᾶς διὰ λουτροῦ παλινγενεσίας
καὶ ἀνακαινώσεως πνεύματος ἁγίου.

For the linguistic parallels see Bauer, *Wörterbuch zum
NT.*, and Büchsel's articles in *Theol. Wörterb. z. NT.*,
i. pp. 663f., 667ff., 685ff.

Amid this variety of expressions we find a group of
closely connected ideas. The metaphor of rebirth is
in some of these passages associated with that of the
Divine "begetting." In some, the regenerated life is
traced to the word of God (*cf.* Luke viii. 11, ὁ σπόρος ἐστιν
ὁ λόγος τοῦ θεοῦ), in others there is an undeniable
allusion to the accompanying rite of baptism. In the
Epistles generally accepted as Pauline the metaphor
is absent, καινὴ κτίσις taking its place (Gal. vi. 15,
2 Cor. v. 17). But even where this Pauline term is not
applied, the Apostle has many allusions to a new life
in the Christian, and in such passages as Rom. vi. 3, 4
this thought is connected with baptism, though the
connection is not of the kind found in Titus iii. 5.

The question to be answered is, How far is the idea
of rebirth, especially with its ritual association, borrowed from Hellenistic religion ?

(1) The idea that a man could be changed into a
"new creature" was not foreign to the old Synagogue,

according to Strack-Billerbeck (*op. cit.* ii. pp. 421f.), who shows that the "new creation" was specially applied when a man experienced renewal : (*a*) in his physical condition by the healing of an infirmity; (*b*) in his outward circumstances by the removal of distress or danger, or (*c*) in his relation to God by the forgiveness of sins. It is of the essence of the new creation that it comes "from above," that is, from God. It should be noted that, according to the rabbinical view, unlike the N.T. teaching, the moral renewing of men belongs only to the future, which alone can bring the new spirit of promise, or the new heart. But while God is spoken of as creator in Judaism, the metaphor is never used in this sense. The one passage in the O.T. which may have contributed to these early Christian ideas is Ps. ii. 7, for the reading of Codex Bezae in Luke iii. 22 shows that the baptism of Jesus was in some quarters interpreted in the light of the words, " Thou art my Son : this day have I begotten thee." It has been suggested that the Messianic experience of Jesus was carried over to the Christian Church and that what was true of Jesus was thought of as in the same way true of every other baptized person. Whilst baptism was regarded as a symbol of cleansing (1 Cor. vi. 11, 1 Pet. iii. 21, Heb. x. 22) such passages as John iii. 5, Tit. iii. 5 and Rom. vi. 4 show that it was also closely associated with the thought of regeneration or an inward renewal. (*Cf.* Herm. *Sim.* IX. xvi. 3–4 : " For before a man bears the name of the Son of God he is dead. But when he receives the seal he puts away mortality and receives life. The seal then is the water. They go down then into the water dead and come up alive.")

(2) The metaphor of Divine " begetting " is frequently found in Philo, who expressly equates γεννᾶν with ποιεῖν and applies it to the creation of the Logos, of the world, and even of animals and of plants. It is used of the relation between God and Adam, and between God and the souls of the Israelites. So God

is the begetter of the reasoning faculty (διάνοια or ὁ λογισμός). Philo even carries the metaphor to daring lengths as in *Ebr.* 30. "The Architect who made this universe was at the same time the father of what was thus born, whilst its mother was the knowledge possessed by its Maker. With his knowledge God had union, not as men have it, and he begat created being. And knowledge having received divine seed, when her travail was consummated, bore the only beloved son, who is apprehended by the senses, the world which we see." The most relevant passages to consult are *Virtut.* 204f., *Conf. Ling.* 63, *Cherub.* 43f., *Vit. Mos.* i. 279, *Mutat. Nom.* 63, 138, *Leg. All.* ii. 47, iii. 180f., 219, *Migr. Abr.* 31, 35, 142, *Post. Cain.* 135, *Quis Rer. Div.* 62, 200, *Op. Mund.* 84, *Somn.* i. 181, *Quod Deus,* 47, *Spec. Leg.* i. 329. These figurative expressions show Philo's contact with the lore of the mysteries, as there is nothing of the kind in his Hebrew or Aramaic sources. But the metaphor of begetting is used either of God's creative activity or of his endowment of men with spiritual, ethical, and religious gifts. He shows no thought of any new birth of man apart from the word. As Büchsel says (*Johannes u.d. hell. Synkret.* p. 61): " God does not beget the man anew, but only something in the man. The thought of the Divine begetting, so far as it is not cosmologically conceived, is clearly allegorized and spiritualized mystery-wisdom." Philo also uses the word παλιγγενεσία (so common with the Stoics and Pythagoreans), but of the three senses in which it is found, (*a*) cosmological, (*b*) national (re-birth after exile, so Josephus, *Ant.* XI. iii. 9 (64)), (*c*) messianic-eschatological (as in Matt. xix. 28), Philo restricts himself to the first. *E.g.* in *Vit. Mos.* ii. 65 (as in 1 Clem. ix. 4) the reference is to the renewal of the world after the flood.

(3) Ever since Reitzenstein's *Die hellenistischen Mys-terienreligionen* first appeared in 1910 there has been a strong tendency to regard the terminology now under consideration as a loan from the numerous mystery

cults, which were even alleged to have provided
Christianity with its sacramental cultus. The best
critical examination of the loosely spun theories of the
new school, so far as it dealt with the Pauline theology,
was H. A. A. Kennedy's *St. Paul and the Mystery Religions* (1913), which is still an invaluable introduction
to the whole subject. It may well be granted that a
missionary religion such as Christianity could not do
other than avail itself of the popular phraseology which
was so widely current in the Hellenistic world. The
deep differences, however, must not be overlooked.
Instead of a short-lived ecstasy, Christianity proclaims
a new life in the Spirit which endures without a
repeatedly renewed regeneration. Christianity does
not develop a special type of esoteric mystic, but proclaims the " open secret " of the Gospel to all. Even
Titus iii. 5, which seems the nearest approximation in
the N.T. to the language of the mysteries, has no
reference to any mystical ecstasy, but explains in the
second and parallel clause that this regeneration is the
continuous working of the power of a new life. Finally,
this regeneration is possible not only to select initiates,
but is regarded as a fundamental experience of all
Christians. On the whole subject see Professor A. D.
Nock's admirable survey in *Essays on the Trinity and the
Incarnation*, pp. 53–156.

(4) In recent times much attention has been paid to
the Hermetic writings (see Lecture II). In the present
connection the most important tractate is Libellus
XIII, which bears the title, λόγος ἀπόκρυφος περὶ
παλιγγενεσίας. See W. Scott's *Hermetica*, i. pp. 238–55
for the Greek text and English translation, ii. pp. 372–
409 for commentary. The Editor dates this tractate
late in the third century A.D. How close the theme is
to that of the conversation between Jesus and Nicodemus may be judged from Mr. Scott's translation of
a passage near the beginning, in which Tat says to
his father : " I know not, thrice greatest one, from what
womb a man can be born again, nor from what seed."

—*Hermes.* My son, the womb is Wisdom, conceiving in silence ; and the seed is the true God.—*Tat.* And who is it, father, that begets ? I am wholly at a loss. —*Hermes.* The will of God, my son, is the begetter.— *Tat.* Tell me this too, who is the ministrant by whom the consummation of the Rebirth is brought to pass ?— *Hermes.* Some man who is a son of God, working in subordination to God's will.—*Tat.* And what manner of man is he that is brought into being by the Rebirth ? —*Hermes.* He that is born by that birth is another ; he is a god, and son of God. He is the All, and is in all ; for he has no part in corporeal substances ; he partakes of the substance of things intelligible, being wholly composed of Powers of God.—*Tat.* Your words are riddles, father ; you do not speak to me as a father to his son."

Scott's judgement (ii. p. 374) is that the doctrine of this tractate is based on Platonism, though not the conception expressed by the term παλιγγενεσία. " The group of Hermetists to which the author of *Corpus* XIII belonged probably got this conception either from the Christians, who held that men are reborn by the sacrament of baptism, or from some Pagan mystery-cult in which men were reborn by a sacramental operation."

See further, on the whole subject, the excursus on John iii. 5 by W. Bauer, that on 1 John iii. 9 by H. Windisch, and that on Tit. iii. 5 by M. Dibelius, in Lietzmann's *Handbuch z. NT*, ed.[3] vi. pp. 51ff., ed.[2] xv. pp. 122f., xiii. p. 94. See also M. Dibelius on James i. 18 in Meyer's *Kommentar*, Der Brief des Jakobus, pp. 99ff.

NOTE C

Eschatology and Mysticism : a Modern Parallel

In Lecture V it has been contended that one who is by temperament and experience a mystic may yet have an eschatological background of thought and that in some of his moods his overwhelming sense of impending crisis may find expression even in apocalyptic imagery. It may not be irrelevant to the argument to adduce an example from a later stage of Christian history, as showing how easily a writer can pass from one of these worlds of thought to another. Let us compare these verses from two Christian hymns.

> Open, Lord, my inward ear,
>   And bid my heart rejoice ;
> Bid my quiet spirit hear
>   Thy comfortable voice ;
> Never in the whirlwind found,
>   Or where earthquakes rock the place,
> Still and silent is the sound,
>   The whisper of Thy grace.
>
> From the world of sin and noise
>   And hurry I withdraw ;
> For the small and inward voice
>   I wait with humble awe ;
> Silent am I now and still,
>   Dare not in Thy presence move ;
> To my waiting soul reveal
>   The secret of Thy love.

That is the prayer of a Christian mystic.

> Come, Thou Conqueror of the nations,
>   Now on Thy white horse appear ;
> Earthquakes, dearths, and desolations
>   Signify Thy kingdom near ;
>   True and faithful !
>   'Stablish Thy dominion here.
>
> Thine the kingdom, power, and glory ;
>   Thine the ransomed nations are :
> Let the heathen fall before Thee,
>   Let the isles Thy power declare ;
>   Judge and conquer
>   All mankind in righteous war.

That is the dialect of undiluted Jewish apocalyptic !
Yet both hymns were written by the same writer,
Charles Wesley. It may be even more surprising to
learn that the first was written in 1742, the second
seventeen years later, in 1759. The reason for the tone
of that apocalyptic ode may be found in the historical
background of the times. In 1750 London was panic
stricken by violent earth-tremors. In 1755 a fearful
earthquake destroyed Lisbon, and the shock was felt
from Scotland to Asia Minor. Then in 1759, the year
when triumphs fell to British arms in every part of
the world, on the very day appointed for the Thanksgiving, eighteen thousand men lay ready to embark
in the French fleet when Admiral Hawke, despite the
shoals and granite reefs of Quiberon Bay, attacked and
destroyed the fleet. To the strained imagination of
the day, the judgements of God might well seem to be
abroad in the earth. Now for anyone who was unaware
of the respective dates when these two hymns were
written, or of the historical events which roused the
expectation of a Divine apocalypse, how easy it would
be to find, in the difference both of vocabulary and of
spiritual mood and tense, cogent arguments against
identity of authorship, or even, if that were grudgingly
conceded, against the true chronological sequence !

The eighteenth-century writer, it may be urged, had
been nurtured on a New Testament which gave
canonical authority to the apocalyptic visions of the
Book of Revelation. But the Fourth Evangelist and
the writer of the First Epistle of St. John had also been
cradled in Jewish apocalyptic and for the first Christian
generation the Book of Daniel had sacred authority.
There is a different emphasis in the eschatology of the
Gospel and the Epistle, and the two books cannot be
compared on equal terms. One is a Gospel, a series
of meditations based on the ministry and teaching of
Jesus, with expansions and interpretations due to long
reflection and repetition in solitude and in a circle of
disciples. The Epistle is a pastoral homily, applying

some of the cardinal truths of the Gospel in view of pressing problems thrust upon the writer by a contemporary situation.   The reference to antichrists, in the appearance of dangerous teachers of false doctrine, may be akin to Paul's Thessalonian reference to the alarming situation produced by Caligula's mad design a few years before, or to Charles Wesley's recrudescence of popular apocalyptic when dangers threatened and the arm of the Lord seemed to be suddenly revealed.

On the subject dealt with in Lecture V, in addition to books and essays mentioned in the footnotes, the following will repay study :

Folke Holmström : *Das eschatologische Denken der Gegenwart*, translated from Swedish into German by Harald Kruska (Gütersloh, 1936).

H. E. Weber : " *Eschatologie* " und " *Mystik* " *im Neuen Testament* (Gütersloh, 1930), together with the review of it by Martin Dibelius in *Deutsche Literaturzeitung*, 29 Mai, 1932.

R. Bultmann : " Die Eschatologie des Johannes-Evangelium " (1928), reprinted in the volume *Glauben und Verstehen* (Tübingen, 1933).

NOTE D

" *Except ye eat the flesh of the Son of Man and drink his blood* " (John vi. 53ff.)

The metaphor of eating and drinking is taken in the Midrash on Eccles. ii. 24, viii. 15 as an allegorical expression for the study of the Torah and the practice of good works.   (Strack-Billerbeck, *op. cit.* ii. p. 485.) For the startling, and for a Jew the repellent, figure in the second clause, the only Jewish parallel which Schlatter can bring forward is Josephus, *B.J.* v. 344 : " For it was still possible to feed upon the public miseries, and to drink of the city's life-blood (καὶ τὸ τῆς πόλεως αἷμα πίνειν)—a picturesque metaphor, but hardly relevant to our purpose.

There is no need to see in these words the Evangelist's reply to second-century slanders about the " Thyestian banquets " of the Christians. Still less are any examples of theophagy culled from Frazer's *Golden Bough* illuminating, and W. Bauer's numerous citations are wide of the mark. The reference is certainly to the Eucharist, but the allusion to the ascension in verses 62–63 makes it clear that the words are not to be interpreted in a material sense.

The Fourth Evangelist was a sacramentalist by temperament, and there is a mystical strain in his sacramental symbolism. But his words are a development of the words of institution as found in our earliest record (1 Cor. xi. 23ff. ; *cf.* Mark xiv. 22–24).

A warning should be given against the emphasis still laid in some modern commentaries on the use of the word τρώγειν. In late Greek this was often used instead of ἐσθίειν as a suppletive to φαγεῖν in the present tense. Thus : (*a*) Matt. xxiv. 38 uses τρώγειν where Luke xvii. 27 has ἐσθίειν in his form of the same logion ; (*b*) John xiii. 18 reads ὁ τρώγων μου τὸν ἄρτον, where the LXX of Ps. xl. 10 (E. V. xli. 9) has ὁ ἐσθίων ἄρτους μου ; (*c*) in mod. Greek τρώγειν is the ordinary word for " eat." See Moulton, *Gr. of N.T. Greek*, ii. p. 238 ; Moulton-Milligan, *Vocab.* p. 644 ; Thumb, *Handb. of Mod. Gr. Vernacular*, pp. 177, 359.

INDEX OF NAMES AND SUBJECTS

INDEX OF GREEK WORDS

INDEX OF HEBREW AND ARAMAIC
WORDS

INDEX OF REFERENCES

OLD TESTAMENT

EARLY CHRISTIAN WRITERS

OTHER ANCIENT WRITERS